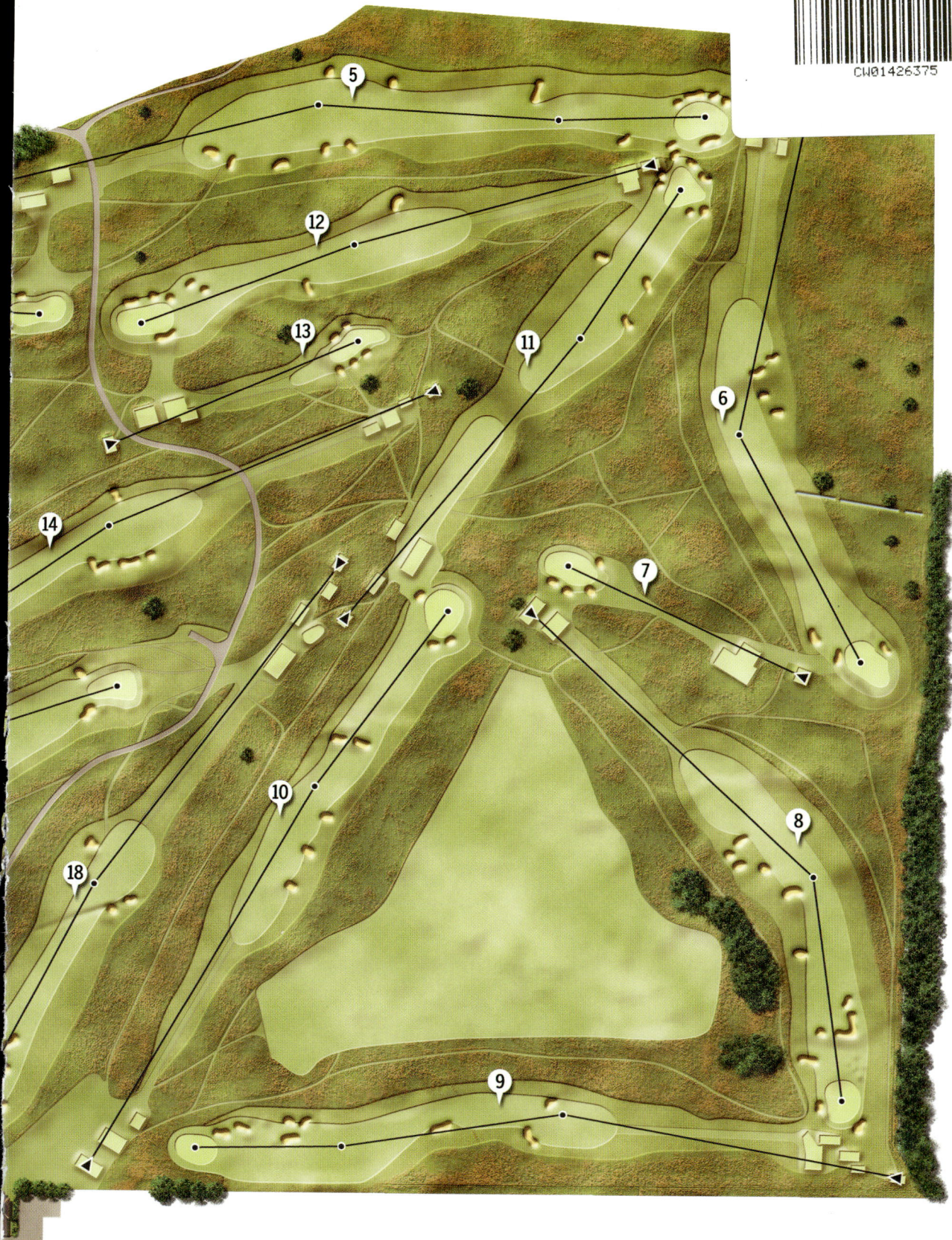

THE OPEN CHAMPIONSHIP

Aurum

Based in St Andrews, The R&A organises
The Open Championship, major amateur
events and international matches. Together
with the United States Golf Association, The
R&A governs the game worldwide, jointly
administering the Rules of Golf, Rules of
Amateur Status, Equipment Standards and
World Amateur Golf Rankings. The R&A's
working jurisdiction is global, excluding
the United States and Mexico.

The R&A is committed to working for golf
and supports the growth of the game
internationally and the development and
management of sustainable golf facilities.
The R&A operates with the consent of 149
organisations from the amateur and
professional game and on behalf of over
thirty million golfers in 135 countries.

R&A

RandA.org

Aurum Press

74-77 White Lion Street, London N1 9PF

Published 2013 by Aurum Press

Course illustration by Graham Gaches

A CIP catalogue record for this book is available
from the British Library

ISBN-13: 978 1 78131 099 1

Designed and produced by Davis Design
Colour retouching by Luciano Retouching Services, Inc.
Printed in the UK by Butler Tanner & Dennis Ltd

THE OPEN CHAMPIONSHIP

EDITOR
Bev Norwood 1947-2013

Bev Norwood was editor of all 30 editions of *The Open Championship Annual* since the publication began with the 1984 Open at St Andrews. He was still working on this edition when cancer claimed him all too quickly. He was 66. He attended over 130 Major Championships and also produced books on the US Open, the Ryder Cup and the Presidents Cup.

A graduate of Wake Forest, Bev first covered The Open in the 1970s as golf writer for the *Winston-Salem Journal*, paying his own way across the Atlantic, before joining Mark McCormack's International Management Group. His roles for IMG included acting as publicist for many of the world's great players, writing for tournament programmes, editing *The World of Professional Golf Annual* and managing the media centre at events such as the Arnold Palmer Invitational at Bay Hill.

Arnold Palmer said: "We will certainly miss his dry wit and the hard work he put into everything he has done for us over the years. He was a great guy and a good friend."

Alastair Johnston, Vice Chairman, IMG, said: "Bev Norwood was a great story teller, but he never wanted to be part of the story. His wit and whimsical sense of humour, that were always so appealing to his friends and colleagues, never left him. For over 30 years Bev served IMG and its golf clients from the 'great and the grand' to the merely mortal as a respected writer and friend in an era before publicists or PR specialists were in vogue."

Peter Dawson, Chief Executive of The R&A, added: "Bev's enthusiasm for The Open was infectious and endured over four decades. His contribution to recording history at this Championship, and others, leaves an outstanding legacy to the game. Many in golf, both inside and outside the media centre, will greatly miss his knowledge, expertise and friendship. We have lost one of our finest."

WRITERS AND PHOTOGRAPHERS

Writers	Getty Images	The R&A	Golf Editors
Andy Farrell	Rob Carr	David Cannon	Rob Harborne
John Hopkins	Stuart Franklin	Ross Kinnaird	Richard Martin-Roberts
Lewine Mair	Matthew Lewis	Warren Little	Steve Rose
Art Spander	Andy Lyons	Mark Runnacles	Mark Trowbridge
Alistair Tait	Andrew Redington	Ian Walton	Maxx Wolfson

The Championship Committee

CHAIRMAN
Jim McArthur

DEPUTY CHAIRMAN
Paul Baxter

COMMITTEE

Stuart Allison	Martin Ebert
Alick Bisset	Stuart Graham
David Boyle	Andrew Stracey
Clive Brown	Peter Unsworth
Tony Disley	David Wybar

CHIEF EXECUTIVE
Peter Dawson

EXECUTIVE DIRECTOR - CHAMPIONSHIPS
Johnnie Cole-Hamilton

EXECUTIVE DIRECTOR - RULES AND EQUIPMENT STANDARDS
David Rickman

Introduction

By Jim McArthur

Chairman of the Championship Committee of The R&A

As always, our aim is straightforward: to provide a true links test for the world's top golfers and to deliver the best spectator experience for golf fans. In terms of the latter, this year we invested in a state-of-the-art Wi-Fi network covering all the main spectator areas and provided four large LED screens offering scoring, statistics and video highlights from around the course. As well as on-site attractions such as The R&A Swing Zone and the HSBC Golf Zone, we also enjoyed The Open in the Square, a three-day public exhibition in St Andrew Square in Edinburgh showcasing The Open and golf in general. Almost 1,000 people received a free golf lesson from a PGA professional and far more posed for a photograph with the Claret Jug.

As for the golf course, it was in outstanding condition. This was the 16th time Muirfield has hosted The Open Championship and, following a few alterations, it again presented a tough but fair challenge to the best golfers in the world. We could not be happier for Phil Mickelson. He is a highly popular Champion after so many years of trying to get to grips with links golf and he won in a thrilling fashion with four birdies over the last six holes. Our congratulations also go to Matthew Fitzpatrick, the reigning Boys Amateur Champion, who won the Silver Medal as the leading amateur at the age of 18.

My thanks go to the Captain, Committee and members of the Honourable Company of Edinburgh Golfers, the greenkeeping staff and all the volunteers whose support and commitment contributed to another outstanding Open Championship.

New Open Champion Phil Mickelson holds the Claret Jug in the company of manager Steve Loy, wife Amy, coach Butch Harmon, caddie Jim "Bones" Mackay, and children Sophia, Evan and Amanda.

Foreword

By Phil Mickelson

The first time I played The Open Championship in 1991 as a 21-year-old amateur, I learned two things. One, that I desperately wanted to love and understand the links game. Two, that it was going to take some time.

I grew up on lush courses in sunny San Diego, California, and played the game in warm air that seldom blew more than 10 miles per hour. As the years went by, trying to adjust to the unpredictable links conditions would prove to be a challenge. I had, of course, always dreamed of being an Open Champion, but was starting to wonder if the Claret Jug would ever be in my grasp. After many years and little success, I knew I had to adjust my game plan and learn to execute shots with less spin and play the game closer to the ground.

Finally, on my 20th try, I was able to develop a strategic plan, hit the necessary shots under pressure, and play the best final round of my career to win the coveted Claret Jug. It's because of this history that winning The Open Championship at the iconic Muirfield in the beloved home of golf is definitely the greatest achievement of my career.

The best moments in life are much sweeter when shared with the people you love. My loving wife Amy and our three kids Amanda, Sophia, and Evan were there on the 18th green with a family hug that I will never forget. Two of my lifelong friends and partners, my agent Steve Loy and my instructor Butch Harmon, were also there to celebrate. And it was especially emotional to share this accomplishment with my good friend and caddie Jim "Bones" Mackay, who has been on my bag and by my side every step of the way since the beginning of my career.

To be introduced as the "Champion Golfer of the Year" and see my name etched on the Claret Jug along with the greatest names in golf is one of the most rewarding moments of my life and more than a dream fulfilled.

The Venue

'Every Shot You Can Imagine'

By Andy Farrell

Victory for Phil Mickelson enhances Muirfield's reputation for identifying top-class Champions.

A great golf course produces great champions. It is a seductive proposition. Often it is true at great Meccas of the game such as St Andrews and Augusta National, though maybe only some of the time. Perhaps only at Muirfield is it true almost all of the time.

To be an Open Champion is special. To be a Muirfield Champion is even more precious. So it was again in 2013. "No matter where it's played, to be able to capture the Claret Jug feels terrific," said Phil Mickelson at the Champion's press conference, before adding: "The past Champions here at Muirfield are exceptional, and to be part of that feels great."

The exceptional list Mickelson joined includes the only British amateur to win The Open twice, Harold Hilton, two of the Great Triumvirate in

Harry Vardon and James Braid, two English knights of the realm, Sir Henry Cotton and Sir Nick Faldo, two of the greatest South Africans the game has seen in Gary Player and Ernie Els, plus four other Americans of notable repute: Walter Hagen, Jack Nicklaus, Lee Trevino and Tom Watson.

This was the 16th time Muirfield has hosted The Open and of the 14 different winners — Braid and Faldo won twice here — 12 are members of the World Golf Hall of Fame, with Mickelson the first to have already been inducted at the time of his victory. Another, Ted Ray, is a notable absentee from the Hall as a winner of an Open at Muirfield and a US Open at Inverness. Which leaves Alf Perry in 1935 as the odd man out. The only Muirfield Champion who is not a multiple Major winner, he was however a staunch member of the golf community, a three-time Ryder Cup player and the long-time professional at Leatherhead Golf Club in Surrey.

By winning the 142nd Open Championship, Mickelson won not only his fifth Major Championship but this third different Major, only six heartbreaking runner-up finishes at the US Open away from

The 15th hole at Muirfield.

Muirfield Champions

Harold Hilton[(A)]	1892
Harry Vardon*	1896
James Braid	1901
James Braid	1906
Ted Ray	1912
Walter Hagen	1929
Alf Perry	1935
Henry Cotton	1948
Gary Player	1959
Jack Nicklaus	1966
Lee Trevino	1972
Tom Watson	1980
Nick Faldo	1987
Nick Faldo	1992
Ernie Els	2002
Phil Mickelson	2013

*Denotes playoff

It's a Fact

Phil Mickelson's 66 is the lowest final round by a Champion at Muirfield. The previous best was 68 by Gary Player in 1959. The lowest 72-hole total is 271 by Tom Watson in 1980.

The grandstand behind the 13th green made for a popular vantage point.

joining the five players who have achieved the career Grand Slam. Nicklaus completed the first of his three sets of Slams at Muirfield in 1966; Player got himself off the mark here in 1959.

If Muirfield loves great Champions, they love it, too. Nicklaus named his course in Columbus, Ohio, Muirfield Village after it. Player named his house after it. Braid gave his son the middle name of Muirfield. Watson, who also won The Senior Open Championship here, said: "I love the place. I love the feel of it, the smell of it, the taste of it. I love the links turf, the feel of my spikes in it. I love everything about it."

On a clear day, the setting is majestic, nestled on prime golf land between Gullane and North Berwick on the shores of the Firth of Forth, with Edinburgh to the west, the North Sea to the east and the Kingdom of Fife to the north. It is home to the Honourable Company of Edinburgh Golfers, who codified the first set of widely distributed Rules of the game in 1744 and joined with Prestwick and The Royal and Ancient in restarting The Open, and providing the Claret Jug, in 1872. After outgrowing first Leith Links and then Musselburgh, the club moved to Muirfield in 1891 and staged its first Open a year later.

It was Harry Colt in the 1920s who revised the course into the layout that is still recognisable today and revered for both its fierceness and also its honesty. Nicklaus called it "challenging" but "inviting" and, overwhelmingly, "fair". "What you see is what you get," he said.

Scottish Walker Cup player Sam McKinlay wrote: "If I had to play a match for my life on a course of my choice, I would plump for Muirfield. It is the best and fairest of courses — not, perhaps, the course where I would choose to play all my golf if my activities had to be restricted to one links, for it is a little too fierce, too long, too exposed to the winds that sweep down Gullane Hill or in from the North Sea. But a man who is in command of his game and himself will fare better at Muirfield than almost any other course I know."

Why is this? Unlike many links built over dramatic sand dunes, and unsurprisingly given its origins as a former racetrack in a stonewall-encircled meadow, there are no blind shots other than the drive at the 11th and the fairway landing areas are generally flat. The bunkers are exceptionally well positioned and the rough at its most penal for the most wayward shots.

According to Pat Ward-Thomas, the late correspondent of *The Guardian*: "The straight, bold stroke rarely, if ever, is in any way seriously punished, but the timid, the gutless and the wayward as rarely will escape retribution. This is surely the mark of a great course."

Another is the requirement to hit many different shots. At Muirfield the first nine circles clockwise and the second nine anticlockwise, with a kink, so the angle to the wind is constantly changing. (Only once, at the third, fourth and fifth, do as many as three successive holes play in the same direction.) Whatever the wind, however, there is a requirement to play some shots high in the air, and others as close to the ground as possible. When the ground is as hard as it was this year, judging how the ball will run when it lands is crucial. Faldo had his old caddie, Fanny Sunesson, bring her yardage books from 1987 and 1992.

The 16th hole is the last par 3 to be negotiated.

The elegant clubhouse of the Honourable Company of Edinburgh Golfers behind the 18th green.

"What we worked out so well in 1992 was where to land the ball 20 yards short of the green, which way it would kick and where it would stop," Faldo recalled. "That's part of the calculations, but you have to hit a solid shot. If you mis-hit, the ball does not react close to what you intend. You look at all the guys who have won here, we hit the ball pretty darn solid."

"Every links shot you can imagine, you're going to play it this week," said defending Champion Els after returning the Claret Jug to The R&A at the start of the week. "It's just a wonderful design. The par 3s are unbelievable, the par 5s have been changed a bit, they're longer. Each and every hole is a little different. There's left-to-rights, right-to-lefts, and it all happens out there."

While a very good player may stick to the shots that serve him or her well, a great player embraces the shots that need hitting at any particular moment and has the skill and the innate self-belief

to execute them. Mickelson did that in his closing 66, the lowest score in the fourth round by a Champion at Muirfield. The left-hander swept to victory with four birdies in the last six holes to avoid the torture many Champions have suffered on the way to victory.

Before this year, four of the previous six winners only triumphed by one stroke and another was forced to extra holes. In 2002, Els had to play a miracle bunker shot at the 13th to save par, but a cruise to victory evaporated when he bogeyed the 14th and had a double-bogey at the 16th. He birdied the 17th but only won a four-way playoff at the fifth extra hole when he made another incredible sand escape at the 18th. "It shows you how close it was to having a really nice win, and then really screwing it up," Els said. "There were a lot of emotions going on."

Faldo famously won in 1987 by grinding out 18 successive pars, but five years later he fell behind

John Cook on the last day and had to play the "best four holes of my life" to triumph. Cook could only say: "I was alive, then I was dead, then I was alive, and then I was very much dead."

In 1972, Trevino looked like making a hash of the 17th hole before he nonchalantly chipped in for a par and a stunned Tony Jacklin three-putted. In 1959, Player had a double-bogey at the last and then had an agonising wait of two hours to find out he had still won, while Cotton skipped a heartbeat when he left a shot in a bunker at the last, but a cool head ensured he still won by five strokes.

Even Hagen's six-stroke victory in 1929 was hard-earned as he returned two rounds of 75 on a day of fierce winds. Mighty storms often blow through this exposed spot and Sandy Lyle played one of the great bad weather rounds, a 71, early on the third morning in 1987. Calm returned for the leaders in the afternoon and it did him little good in the grand scheme of things. In 2002, it was on the Saturday afternoon that hell arrived with a vengeance and Tiger Woods went round in 81, the worst score of his professional career. A 65 the next day could not salvage his quest for a third successive Major victory.

For the 2013 Championship, only the seventh, 13th and 16th holes, all par 3s, were unaltered from 11 years earlier. New tees were installed at seven holes, adding 158 yards to the course, and most holes either had new bunkers added or others relocated to make the entrances to the greens tighter.

"Muirfield is often described as a fair but tough Championship test," said Jim McArthur, Chairman of the Championship Committee, on the eve of the event. "We are confident it will continue to test the best players of today, just as it tested the players of yesterday. The greatest golfers of every era have won here in the past and we're sure that this year's winner will also be in the top-class category."

Digital Evolution at The Open

Digital technology at The Open Championship is bringing exciting opportunities to spectators attending the event and to those watching around the world on television or online. The digital evolution at The Open does not end with web sites and apps. A number of other innovations are being introduced to improve the spectator experience. Manual scoreboards have long been dotted around the course. This year for the first time they were complemented by LED scoreboards — on the seventh, 13th, 16th and 17th holes — to provide more up-to-date and wide-ranging digital content. This included live and recorded video highlights, scoring, statistics, and player and venue information.

Exempt Competitors

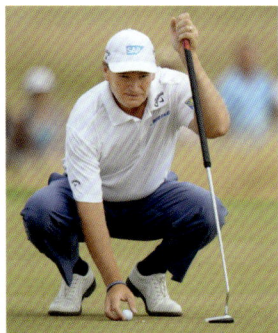

Name, Country	Category	Name, Country	Category
Thomas Aiken, South Africa	4	Tom Lehman, USA	1
Thomas Bjorn, Denmark	8	Marc Leishman, Australia	5
Jonas Blixt, Sweden	5	Justin Leonard, USA	1,3
Keegan Bradley, USA	5,12,14,17	Shane Lowry, Republic of Ireland	6
Angel Cabrera, Argentina	11	Sandy Lyle, Scotland	1
Rafael Cabrera-Bello, Spain	6	David Lynn, England	5,6
Mark Calcavecchia, USA	1,3,4	Hunter Mahan, USA	5,14
KJ Choi, Korea	13	Matteo Manassero, Italy	5,6,7
Stewart Cink, USA	1,2,3	Graeme McDowell, Northern Ireland	4,5,6,10,17
Tim Clark, South Africa	5	Rory McIlroy, Northern Ireland	5,6,10,12,14,17
Darren Clarke, Northern Ireland	1,2,3	Phil Mickelson, USA	5,11,14,17
George Coetzee, South Africa	6	Francesco Molinari, Italy	5,6,17
Nicolas Colsaerts, Belgium	4,5,6,17	Ryan Moore, USA	5,14
Fred Couples, USA	25	Alexander Noren, Sweden	4,6
Ben Curtis, USA	1,2,3	Geoff Ogilvy, Australia	4
Jason Day, Australia	5	Thorbjorn Olesen, Denmark	4,5,6
Graham DeLaet, Canada	5	Mark O'Meara, USA	1
Luke Donald, England	4,5,6,7,14,17	Louis Oosthuizen, South Africa	1,2,3,5,6,14
Jamie Donaldson, Wales	5,6	Carl Pettersson, Sweden	5,14
Jason Dufner, USA	5,14,17	Scott Piercy, USA	5,14
Ken Duke, USA	5	DA Points, USA	5
David Duval, USA	1	Garrick Porteous*, England	26
Ernie Els, South Africa	1,2,3,4,5,14	Ian Poulter, England	4,5,6,17
Harris English, USA	15	Rhys Pugh*, Wales	28
Sir Nick Faldo, England	1	Richie Ramsay, Scotland	6
Gonzalo Fernandez-Castano, Spain	5,6	Justin Rose, England	5,6,10,14,17
Rickie Fowler, USA	5,14	Brett Rumford, Australia	8
Steven Fox*, USA	27	Charl Schwartzel, South Africa	5,6,11
Marcus Fraser, Australia	6	Adam Scott, Australia	4,5,11,14
Hiroyuki Fujita, Japan	22	John Senden, Australia	14
Jim Furyk, USA	5,14,17	Peter Senior, Australia	19
Stephen Gallacher**, Scotland	5	Marcel Siem, Germany	6
Sergio Garcia, Spain	5,14,17	Webb Simpson, USA	5,10,14,17
Robert Garrigus, USA	5,14	Vijay Singh, Fiji	4
Lucas Glover, USA	10	Brandt Snedeker, USA	4,5,14,17
Branden Grace, South Africa	5,6,20	Jordan Spieth, USA	16
Bill Haas, USA	5	Scott Stallings, USA	5
Todd Hamilton, USA	1,2	Kyle Stanley, USA	5
Peter Hanson, Sweden	5,6,17	Henrik Stenson, Sweden	5
Padraig Harrington, Republic of Ireland	1,2,3,12	Richard Sterne, South Africa	8
Russell Henley, USA	15	Kevin Streelman, USA	5
Billy Horschel, USA	15	Toru Taniguchi, Japan	22
John Huh, USA	14	Michael Thompson, USA	5
Mikko Ilonen, Finland	8	Bo Van Pelt, USA	5,14
Makoto Inoue, Japan	23	Jimmy Walker, USA	15
Fredrik Jacobson, Sweden	5	Marc Warren, Scotland	8
Thongchai Jaidee, Thailand	5,6	Nick Watney, USA	5,14
Miguel Angel Jimenez, Spain	4,6	Bubba Watson, USA	5,11,14,17
Dustin Johnson, USA	4,5,14,17	Tom Watson, USA	3
Zach Johnson, USA	4,5,14,17	Boo Weekley, USA	15
Brendan Jones, Australia	23	Lee Westwood, England	5,6,14,17
Shingo Katayama, Japan	23	Bernd Wiesberger, Austria	6
Martin Kaymer, Germany	5,6,12,17	Danny Willett, England	6
Hyung-Sung Kim, Korea	24	Thaworn Wiratchant, Thailand	18
KT Kim, Korea	23	Chris Wood, England	5
Satoshi Kodaira, Japan	24	Tiger Woods, USA	1,2,3,4,5,13,14,17
Kenichi Kuboya, Japan	21	YE Yang, Korea	12
Matt Kuchar, USA	4,5,13,14,17		
Martin Laird, Scotland	5		
Paul Lawrie, Scotland	1,5,6,17		

* Denotes amateurs   ** Denotes reserve

Ernie Els

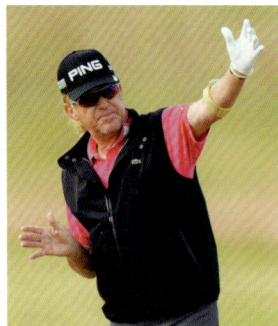

Miguel Angel Jimenez

Brandt Snedeker

Lee Westwood

Justin Leonard

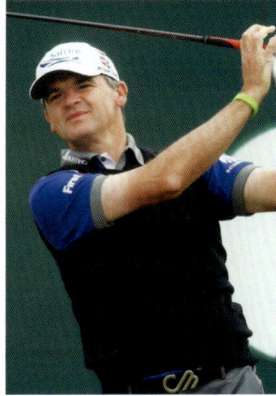
Paul Lawrie

Jason Day

Sir Nick Faldo

Key to Exemptions from Regional, Local Final and International Final Qualifying

Exemptions for 2013 were granted to the following:

(1)   The Open Champions aged 60 or under on 21 July 2013.

(2)   The Open Champions for 2003-2012.

(3)   The Open Champions finishing in the first 10 and tying for 10th place in The Open Championship 2008-2012.

(4)   First 10 and anyone tying for 10th place in the 2012 Open Championship at Royal Lytham & St Annes.

(5)   The first 50 players on the Official World Golf Ranking for Week 21, Sunday 26 May 2013.

(6)   First 30 in the Race to Dubai for 2012.

(7)   The BMW PGA Championship winners for 2011-2013.

(8)   First 5 European Tour members and any European Tour members tying for 5th place, not otherwise exempt, in the top 20 of the Race to Dubai on completion of the 2013 Alstom Open de France.

(9)   The Scottish Open Champion 2013.

(10) The US Open Champions for 2009-2013.

(11) The Masters Tournament Champions for 2009-2013.

(12) The PGA Champions for 2008-2012.

(13) The PLAYERS Champions for 2011-2013.

(14) The leading 30 qualifiers for the 2012 TOUR CHAMPIONSHIP.

(15) First 5 PGA TOUR members and any PGA TOUR members tying for 5th place, not exempt, in the top 20 of the PGA TOUR FedExCup Points List for 2013 on completion of the 2013 Greenbrier Classic.

(16) The John Deere Classic winner 2013.

(17) Playing members of the 2012 Ryder Cup teams.

(18) First and anyone tying for 1st place on the Order of Merit of the Asian Tour for 2012.

(19) First and anyone tying for 1st place on the Order of Merit of the Tour of Australasia for 2012.

(20) First and anyone tying for 1st place on the Order of Merit of the Southern Africa PGA Sunshine Tour for 2012.

(21) The Japan Open Champion for 2012.

(22) First 2 and anyone tying for 2nd place on the Official Money List of the Japan Golf Tour for 2012.

(23) The leading 4 players, not exempt, in the 2013 Mizuno Open. With the exception of ties for first place, which will be determined in accordance with the Conditions for the tournament concerned, ties will be decided in favour of the highest Official World Golf Ranking player at the commencement of the tournament.

(24) First 2 and anyone tying for 2nd place, not exempt having applied 23 above, in a cumulative money list taken from all official 2013 Japan Golf Tour events up to and including the 2013 Mizuno Open.

(25) The Senior Open Champion for 2012.

(26) The Amateur Champion for 2013.

(27) The US Amateur Champion for 2012.

(28) The European Amateur Champion for 2012.

(29) The Mark H McCormack Medal (Men's World Amateur Golf Ranking) winner for 2012.

(26) to (29) were only applicable if the entrant concerned was still an amateur on 18 July 2013.

International Final Qualifying

AMERICA — 20 May

Gleneagles — *Plano, Texas*

Josh Teater, USA	64	69	133
Johnson Wagner, USA	68	66	134
Camilo Villegas, Colombia	68	66	134
Scott Brown, USA	71	64	135
Brian Davis, England	66	69	135
Robert Karlsson[(P)], Sweden	67	69	136
Luke Guthrie[(P)], USA	65	71	136
Bud Cauley[(P)], USA	70	66	136

[(P)] Qualified after playoff

Josh Teater

ASIA — 28 February & 1 March

Amata Spring — *Bangkok, Thailand*

Kiradech Aphibarnrat, Thailand	68	63	131
Hideki Matsuyama[(A)], Japan	66	69	135
Daisuke Maruyama, Japan	71	65	136
Ashun Wu, China	68	68	136

Kiradech Aphibarnrat

AUSTRALASIA — 29 & 30 January

Kingston Heath — *Melbourne, Australia*

Mark Brown, New Zealand	72	62	134
Steven Jeffress, Australia	68	67	135
Stephen Dartnall, Australia	67	69	136

Mark Brown

EUROPE   24 June

Sunningdale   *Berkshire, England*

Brooks Koepka, USA	69	65	134
Oliver Fisher, England	70	65	135
Alvaro Quiros, Spain	70	66	136
Gregory Bourdy, France	68	68	136
Richard McEvoy, England	71	65	136
Gareth Maybin, N. Ireland	67	69	136
Niclas Fasth, Sweden	68	69	137
Scott Jamieson, Scotland	71	66	137
Estanislao Goya[(P)], Argentina	68	70	138

[(P)] Qualified after playoff

Brooks Koepka

Muirfield ★

AFRICA   5 & 6 March

Royal Johannesburg   *Johannesburg,*
& Kensington   *South Africa*

Justin Harding, South Africa	66	64	130
Eduardo De La Riva, Spain	67	66	133
Darryn Lloyd, South Africa	66	69	135

Justin Harding

Local Final Qualifying

Dunbar

Grant Forrest*, Scotland	67 65	132
Shiv Kapur, India	69 64	133
John Wade, Australia	70 63	133

Gullane No 1

Ben Stow*, England	72 68	140
Oscar Floren, Sweden	72 69	141
Matthew Fitzpatrick*, England	69 72	141

North Berwick

Jimmy Mullen*, England	68 68	136
Gareth Wright(P), Wales	69 68	137
George Murray(P), Scotland	73 64	137

The Musselburgh

Steven Tiley, England	64 69	133
Lloyd Saltman, Scotland	68 68	136
Tyrrell Hatton, England	69 67	136

* Denotes amateurs   (P) Qualified after playoff

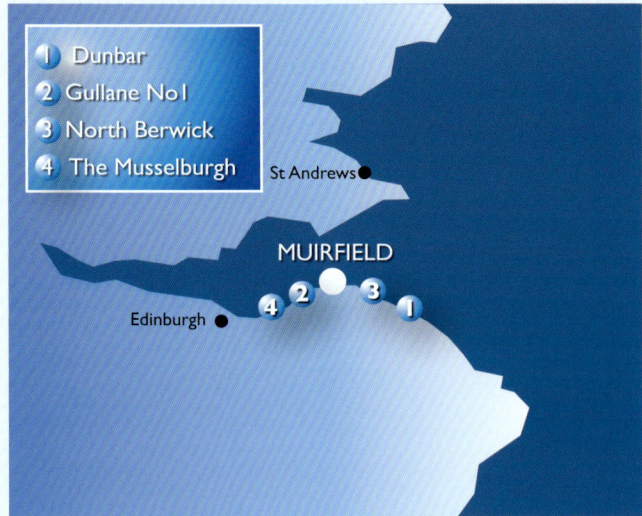

1 Dunbar
2 Gullane No1
3 North Berwick
4 The Musselburgh

St Andrews

MUIRFIELD

Edinburgh

The Starting Field (from Entry Form)

"In the event of an exempt player withdrawing from the Championship or further places becoming available in the starting field after the close of entries, these places will be allocated in the ranking order of entrants from OWGR (Official World Golf Ranking) at the time that intimation of withdrawal is received or further places are made available by the Championship Committee. Any withdrawals following issue of OWGR Week 27 will be taken in ranking order from OWGR Week 27."

Stephen Gallacher, Scotland, replaced John Daly, USA

Grant Forrest

Matthew Fitzpatrick

Jimmy Mullen

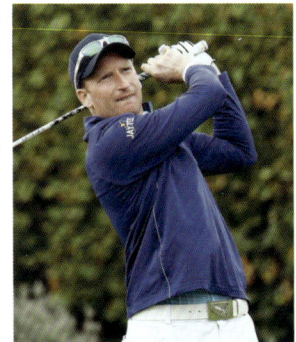

Steven Tiley

Practice Days

Ian Poulter with son Joshua.

Tom Watson received the Spirit of Golf award from the Golf Foundation.

Justin Rose and Sir Nick Faldo.

Rory McIlroy won the Golf Writers Trophy.

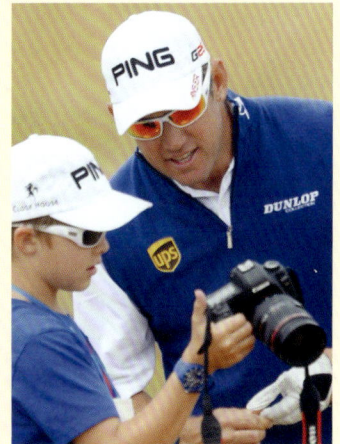

Lee Westwood with son Sam.

Ernie Els returned the Claret Jug to Peter Dawson, Chief Executive of The R&A.

THE OPEN CHAMPIONSHIP

First Round

Look at the Old Man

By Andy Farrell

Mark O'Meara leads an eclectic group trailing Zach Johnson on an opening day of lightning-fast greens at Muirfield.

A long, hot day under the Scottish sun that left Muirfield as treacherous a links as has been experienced in an Open Championship for many a year, also produced the most wonderfully eclectic first-round leaderboard. Unexpected guests among the leading contenders are *de rigueur* on the opening day of an Open, but the 142nd edition appeared to have all bases covered.

Of the 14 players who broke 70, seven were Major Champions (four of them Open Champions) and of the other seven, one had come through Local Final Qualifying and another had only earned an exemption by winning a tournament the previous Sunday. In fact, two had won the week before, another had lost in a playoff. Five of the group were in the top 30 of the Official World Golf Ranking,

Mark O'Meara, 56, "felt like I was 32 again" after his 67.

including numbers one and five, and four were outside the top 200.

One was a teenager (at least for another week or so), two were in their 20s, five in their 30s, four in their 40s and two in their 50s. Six took advantage on the easier first nine, but the other eight all scored lower on the harder inward half. Nine were Americans but the others were an Indian, an Argentinean and two Spaniards. Even the Spaniards could not be more different, one a pony-tailed, cigar-smoking 49-year-old who broke his leg skiing in the winter, the other a strappingly athletic 29-year-old from the tiny island of Gran Canaria who likes surfing.

Of all these stories, perhaps the most romantic belonged to Mark O'Meara. "I didn't feel like I was 56 years old out there today," said the 1998 Champion, "I felt like I was 32." If his long putt at the last had fallen in, rather than lipping out, O'Meara would have matched the 66 of Zach Johnson, whose five-under round led the way. Another old Champion, Tom Lehman, from 1996 at Royal Lytham, did hole a monster putt on the final green for a 68, while Todd Hamilton, the 2004 winner

1

First Round • 23

Australian Peter Senior had the honour of teeing-off first.

from Royal Troon, was among those on 69.

It was a day for experience, except that Rafael Cabrera-Bello who, after a 67, was one better than his mentor, Miguel Angel Jimenez, and India's Shiv Kapur, who scored a 68, were playing in only their second Opens. And Jordan Spieth, who had a 69, was playing in his first after beating Zach Johnson and David Hearn in a playoff to win the John Deere Classic on the PGA Tour and claim a last-minute trip to Scotland.

For the record, the others filling out the top of the leaderboard were Dustin Johnson and Brandt Snedeker on 68, and Angel Cabrera and Francesco Molinari on 69 along with Tiger Woods and Phil Mickelson.

When O'Meara arrived at the 10th tee after birdieing the ninth to get to five under, Woods was crossing just in front of the tee to go to the practice putting green. "I hadn't seen him since

Rafael Cabrera-Bello, in his second Open, was one off the lead.

Zach Johnson putted beautifully to take the lead on 66.

First Round Leaders

HOLE	1	2	3	4	5	6	7	8	9	10	11	12	13	14	15	16	17	18	
PAR	4	4	4	3	5	4	3	4	5	4	4	4	3	4	4	3	5	4	TOTAL
Zach Johnson	4	4	③	3	❸	③	②	4	5	4	4	③	3	[5]	4	3	5	4	66
Rafael Cabrera-Bello	4	③	4	②	④	4	3	4	[6]	4	③	4	②	4	[5]	3	④	4	67
Mark O'Meara	③	③	4	3	④	③	3	4	④	[5]	4	4	3	[5]	[5]	3	❸	4	67

Miguel Angel Jimenez birdied the first three holes just months after breaking his leg while skiing.

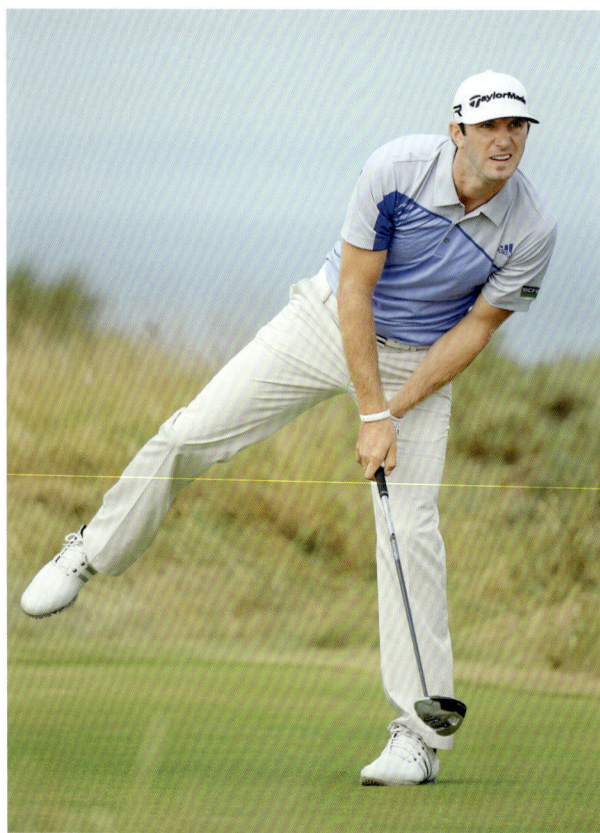

Dustin Johnson was two behind that other Johnson, Zach.

the Masters but he gave me a wink," O'Meara said. "And I got up and piped my drive on 10 and to do that in front of him was a good feeling."

His day had got off to the best of starts when he birdied the first two holes from three and a half and three feet respectively, and holed from 11 feet on the sixth to go with two other birdies at the par 5s. After the fine drive on the 10th, he found a greenside bunker to drop the first of three shots that were all caused by finding sand. A 35-footer for eagle at the 17th, however, quickly restored his good mood. "That was the highlight of the day because I needed a shot in the arm," he said. "I thought the putt at the last was tracking, but it was a tough two-putt, so a birdie would have been a bonus."

Suddenly, O'Meara was not simply marking time for the following week's Senior Open Championship at his beloved Royal Birkdale but right in contention. "Can I win? I hope my wife thinks I've got a chance of winning because I'm building a new house," he said.

Brandt Snedeker recovered from a double-bogey at the sixth to post a 68.

O'Meara's passion for The Open and links golf comes pouring out when he gets talking. Before leaving on a trip such as this, he hides his replica Claret Jug and Masters trophy for safekeeping. "When I picked up the Claret Jug the other day to put it somewhere special in my house, I realised that no matter what happens for the rest of my life, my name is on that trophy at least one time. Whether it will happen again or not, that would be a dream come true. But I take tremendous pride in the fact I've won The Open Championship, because to me this is *the* Championship."

He added: "Links golf is a little different than playing in the Masters. It's a little bit different to playing in the US Open, or the PGA. From the standpoint that experience plays a big factor in how

1

Tom Lehman was another former Champion to enjoy a fine day.

guys play. Links golf is not just about power, where a lot of the game today is bombs away, hit the ball a long way up in the air. Links golf is about creativity, shot process, thinking about where you need to land the ball. Links golf is so much more enjoyable and what golf should be like."

Not everyone was quite so enamoured of the joys of links golf. "Joy would not be the word I'd use to describe it, no," said Mickelson. It was a day where the frustrations of playing such a demanding course as Muirfield at its most firm and fast were understandably apparent.

Not since Hoylake in 2006 had players arrived at such a dry venue

Phil Mickelson at the 14th, where he would make a birdie, during a 69.

for an Open. Early overcast skies soon burnt off and the course baked under the full force of the sun and a 10mph breeze. The fairways went from green to brown, and the greens from brown to white. Although the greens were like lightning in the afternoon, it was perhaps the morning players who had to adapt more as their rounds went on. Everyone is used to conditions changing during the day on a links, wind or rain picking up or calming down, but the way the course quickened up so rapidly caught many by surprise.

Under the circumstances, it was natural that some of the more testing pin positions should draw comment. Ian Poulter tweeted in his usual understated manner that, "the eighth was a joke & the 18th needs a windmill and a clown face." The only crazy golf around was Poulter's four bogeys in the last five holes, including a lip-out for par at the last, which dropped him back to a 72.

Mickelson also bogeyed the last, though two brilliant approaches at the 14th and 15th holes suggested a mastery of the final six holes of the course which would hold him in good stead throughout the

It's a
Fact

The 66s of Zach Johnson in round one and by Phil Mickelson in round four were the lowest scores of the week. The last time 66 was the low score of the Championship at Muirfield was in 1987 when it was achieved by Payne Stewart and Ross Drummond in round two.

1

First Round Scores	
Players Under Par	20
Players At Par	6
Players Over Par	128

Tiger Woods made a par from this bunker at the 12th and came home in 32.

2004 Champion Todd Hamilton was the first player to break 70.

week. "I got very lucky to play early today, because as the day wore on and we got on the back nine, about a third of every green seemed to die and become brown," Mickelson said. "The pins were very edgy, on the slopes and what not, so the guys who played early had a huge break. Even without any wind it's beyond difficult."

On behalf of The R&A, Chief Executive Peter Dawson responded: "We set up the golf course to test players' course management strategy as much as anything. We are very happy with the scoring, five under par is about where we expected the lead to be. It's far from unplayable, but we do hear players' comments and we're not so insular as to ignore it."

Zach Johnson teed-off at 10.06, 22 minutes after Mickelson, Rory McIlroy and Hideki Matsuyama,

Round of the Day: Zach Johnson - 66

OFFICIAL SCORECARD
THE OPEN CHAMPIONSHIP 2013
MUIRFIELD

Zach JOHNSON
Game 20
Thursday 18 July at 10:06am

FOR R&A USE ONLY

ROUND 1
18 HOLE TOTAL

THIS ROUND 66   66

VERIFIED 197

ROUND 1

Hole	1	2	3	4	5	6	7	8	9	Out	10	11	12	13	14	15	16	17	18	In	Total
Yards	447	364	377	226	559	461	184	441	554	3613	469	387	379	190	475	448	186	575	470	3579	7192
Par	4	4	4	3	5	4	3	4	5	36	4	4	4	3	4	4	3	5	4	35	71
Score	4	4	3	3	3	3	2	4	5	31	4	4	3	3	5	4	3	5	4	35	66

Signature of Marker

Signature of Competitor
Zach Johnson

Noteworthy

- **Hole 3**: 3-iron, wedge, one putt from five feet
- **Hole 5**: Driver, 5-iron, one putt from 45 feet
- **Hole 6**: 3-wood, 9-iron, one putt from 15 feet
- **Hole 7**: 5-iron, one putt from nine feet
- **Hole 12**: 3-iron, 8-iron, one putt from 20 feet
- **Hole 14**: 3-wood, 4-iron, bunker, two putts from 45 feet

and, as Mickelson suggested, his lead stood up all day. "There are some dicey pins out there and it's not going to get any easier as the day goes on," Johnson said. "Granted it's easy for me to stand up here because I shot the lowest score so far and say I enjoyed the course, but I can see what some guys are saying. The course is very baked. It's playable but you really have to pay attention around the hole. What you have to pay attention to is the colour. If it's green, it's a little slower. If it's brown, it's going to continue to roll."

Lee Westwood, one of the afternoon starters who returned a 72, described how on the 13th green he thought he had left a putt 10 feet short and it went 16 feet past. "So I was 26 feet out with my feel," he said. "That tells you the greens are getting tricky."

Woods, who was playing for the first time since the US Open due to an elbow injury, made three birdies in the first four holes of the second nine thanks to a magical putter but at the 14th putted the full length of the green and rolled off the back. "It really wasn't that bad a putt," he said. "I could see how guys were complaining about it. As the golf course dried out, it got quick."

O'Meara had the last word on the conditions. "I've stood on holes where it's 200 or so yards and hit driver, and I could barely hold onto the club and it's freezing, raining and sleeting and cold and

"Top golfers moaning about tough conditions are about as likely to draw sympathy as Premier League footballers complaining about income tax, as Ian Poulter discovered yesterday when his criticism of Muirfield drew a mixed reception, even from within the locker room."

—Matt Dickinson, *The Times*

"Tiger Woods ... took the last Open played on such a brown palette, at Hoylake in 2006, and is now well-positioned to end his Major Championship victory drought which has entered its sixth year. But first he needs to learn to handle the first hole."

—Alan Shipnuck, Golf.com

"Watch McIlroy take a full cut at the ball and you'd still give up the family inheritance to have that swing. But he's 24 over par in the Majors this year and he's only played nine rounds."

—Ron Green Jr, *Global Golf Post*

"On a baking hot day when the temperature touched 30 degrees, O'Meara demonstrated to some of the feather-bedded youngsters on tour how to handle a course in real links condition. And it wasn't the British — supposedly more used to bump-and-run golf — who flourished in this hottest Open since Hoylake in 2006. It was the Americans."

—Jock MacVicar, *Daily Express*

In the Words of the Competitors…

"

"There's even less pressure than there was before. I kind of accomplished more than I'd thought possible this year."

—Jordan Spieth

"When you're struggling with your long game around a course like this, there's no let-up. Each tee you're standing on is just a battle."

—Oliver Fisher

"Championship golf is like that — sometimes it's not fair to everybody. It's very difficult to make a golf course like that."

—Lee Westwood

"I really love links golf. I think it gets all the imagination out of a player."

—Rafael Cabrera-Bello

"To be honest, this is more what I like. Last week I said the greens weren't fast enough. It's definitely not an issue this week."

—Martin Laird

"I couldn't single out a pin that I thought was unfair. But if you got on the wrong side of them, they could make you look very, very silly."

—Graeme McDowell

"

Francesco Molinari birdied the 17th hole during an inward 33.

I couldn't put my umbrella up. To me that's way more miserable than what we had out there. I thought it was tough, challenging, but unfair, no. If they think it's that way, they need to look at the old man and say, how did he do it? Seriously. Guys are good, they should be able to play in these conditions."

It was Peter Senior, the 53-year-old Australian Open champion, who was the first to tee-off at 6.32am, but it was his playing partner, Lloyd Saltman, who made the dramatic start. Saltman, who lives just down the road from Muirfield, hit his first two drives out of bounds and ended up with an 8. Others to struggle at the first included Thomas Bjorn, whose second shot from the rough went

Oliver Fisher, in the first group out, battled his way to a 70.

Jordan Spieth, 19, enjoyed a fine Open debut with a 69.

Shiv Kapur

'The Best Nine Holes of My Life'

Not all members of the media were as thrilled for Shiv Kapur as they should have been as he set off into the evening sun — 15.40 to be precise — on Thursday.

The writers' tales of how Zach Johnson was leading the field from Rafael Cabrera-Bello and the 56-year-old Mark O'Meara were at the polishing stage, but, as Kapur, the 31-year-old Indian, swept across the slippery links in a succession of birdies, so their stories had to go on hold. There was a very good chance that they would need more than a spot of re-jigging.

Kapur, who had qualified for only his second Open at Dunbar but enjoyed a Muirfield primer thanks to a practice round in the company of Sir Nick Faldo, had started out with four 3s, the first three of which were birdies. He then followed up with a sequence of 4-3-2 against the par of 5-4-3 to be as many as six under after seven on his way to turning in 30.

The greens were a shimmering white and Kapur's touch golden as one putt after another bolted for home and took him to the top of the leaderboard.

As the party set off down the 10th fairway, so one of Kapur's playing companions made laughing reference to how he had hoped for a quiet afternoon, "and now look what you've done to me with all the cameras!"

Heaven knows how the psychologists describe what happens between holing a putt at the ninth and standing on the 10th tee, but for Kapur, no less than many another, it proved a turning point.

His drive had finished in a bunker and, though he recovered well, he knocked his third some 12 feet past the hole before walking from the green with a three-putt, double-bogey-6. There was another mishap at the 14th — this time a bogey rather than a double — where he pulled his drive into the left rough.

He never retrieved any of those three dropped shots, but at the end of a day which came to a halt with a second well worthy of the members' stares from the clubhouse window, he was far from unhappy with a three-under 68.

Kapur may not have held the attention of all the media, but what he had done would have resonated with youngsters all over India. "If you have someone go out and do well in a Major it gives Indian kids a lot of belief," said the player, who added every Indian golfer longed to be the guy who was setting the bar for the children at home.

In spite of his less-glamorous second nine, Kapur bedded down a happy man. He had played "probably the best nine holes of my life" in just about the finest setting in golf. Over the next three days he would visit too many bunkers to stay in contention and eventually finished tied for 73rd.

"At least," he said, "I can hold my head up high and say 'I led The Open Championship.'"

—Lewine Mair

Bubba Watson visited the notorious Muirfield rough but returned with a 70.

straight through the lens of an ESPN television camera, and Woods, who hit a lone bush on the left and had to take an unplayable.

No such problems for Jimenez, who made the early running by birdieing the first three holes and went out in 31. He dropped a couple of shots coming home, but it was a remarkable round considering he was suffering from tennis elbow and was still not quite recovered from breaking his leg in the winter while skiing. His young compatriot, Cabrera-Bello, birdied the 13th to get to four under and recovered the shot he dropped at the 15th with a two-putt birdie at the 17th.

Snedeker came home in 32, a return which was only equalled by Woods later in the day. Snedeker was playing with the new US Open Champion, Justin Rose, who struggled to a 75, and Ernie Els. After winning at Royal Lytham in 2012, the South African was the sixth player to be defending the title at a venue at which he had won the last time The Open was played there. The only other occurrence at

Excerpts FROM THE Press

"They say Muirfield is the fairest of the courses used in The Open Championship rotation. This is true. But that does not mean it can't leave teeth marks on your round."

—Gene Wojciechowski, *ESPN.com*

"Martin Laird revealed he had great fun on firm and fiery Muirfield as he played his way into Open contention. Laird was one of just a handful of players to score under par in the afternoon groups and he admitted the harder the course seemed to get the more he enjoyed it."

—Robert Martin, *The Sun*

"He prepared for this tournament by reading *Zen Golf: Mastering the Mental Game*, and picked up a few tips on plotting one's way around a links course during an 11th-hour practice round with Sir Nick Faldo. For much of the day, Shiv Kapur played like England's six-time Major Champion in his pomp."

—Tom Cary, *The Daily Telegraph*

"Graeme McDowell refused to blame the tough pins or slick greens as he slid to a three-over 75 at slippery Muirfield."

—Brian Keogh, *Irish Golf Desk*

"Watson is a freak of nature. No more, no less. He almost won this thing four years ago at Turnberry, aged 59. He won't win it at 63 but his ball-striking is sublime. You can stand three feet away from Watson and you don't hear the ball leave his club."

—David McCarthy, *Daily Record*

1

Masters Champion Adam Scott opened with a 71.

Ken Duke eagled the 17th for a 70.

Amateur Jimmy Mullen posted a 71.

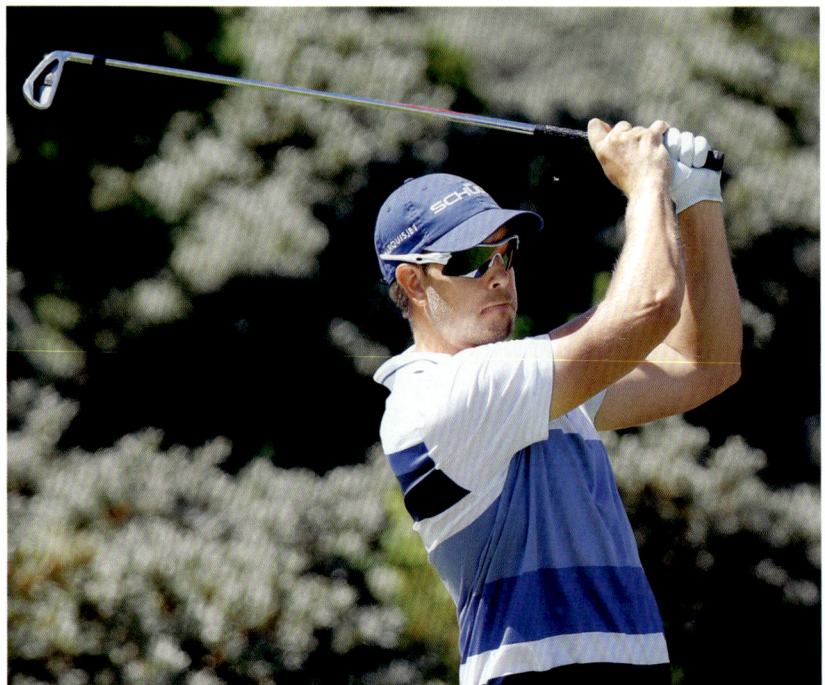

Henrik Stenson, on one under, continued his fine form from the Scottish Open.

Muirfield was James Braid in 1906, who promptly won again. Els would not match him. In contrast to his stellar bunker play at Muirfield in 2002, Els left two balls in the sand at the 16th, costing him a triple-bogey-6 and a round of 74.

Zach Johnson, like Jimenez and O'Meara, went out in 31 and enjoyed a stunning sequence of four 3s and a 2 from the third hole. The run included an eagle at the fifth when he rolled in a curling 45-footer. At the third and the seventh he holed from under five feet, and although he got to six under with a 20-footer at the 12th, he dropped a shot at the 14th after finding a bunker.

Johnson was lying second after an opening 65 at Lytham in 2012, so he has obviously found a good routine for preparing for The Open. It involves playing at the John Deere Classic in America, where he led for much of the final round before losing the playoff, and then getting on the charter plane with other players to Edinburgh. He played nine holes on Monday, 18 on Tuesday and nine again on Wednesday, while otherwise he was hanging

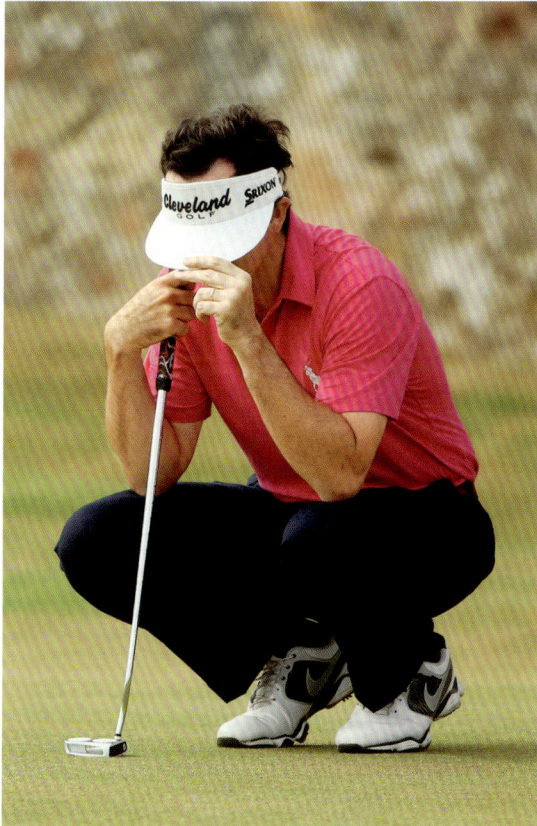

Don't look now, Gonzalo Fernandez-Castano on 70.

Ian Poulter expressed his frustrations but was handily placed on 72.

out in his rented house with 2009 Champion Stewart Cink and their two caddies. "I don't know if there is a perfect formula, but I've got mine and it's worked somewhat as of late," he said.

"What I've embraced from last week is that I'm playing great and I'm confident in what I'm doing. I'm confident in my routines, I'm confident in my walk and I'm confident in my lines. Any time you shoot under par in a Major, you must be putting decent and I putted great."

It was the 19-year-old Spieth who won the John Deere Classic, becoming the first teenager to win on the PGA Tour since Ralph Guldahl in 1931. He had only packed for one week when he went to the AT&T National at Congressional but finished high enough to play the next week at the Greenbrier and then went straight on to the John Deere before jumping on the charter after his victory got him into The Open. Fortunately, his family arrived in Scotland with some extra clothes, while he already had experience of links golf from the Junior Open at Hesketh in 2008 and the Walker Cup at Royal Aberdeen in 2011.

Low Scores	
Low First Nine	
Shiv Kapur	30
Low Second Nine	
Brandt Shedeker	32
Tiger Woods	32
Low Round	
Zach Johnson	66

①

Round One Hole Summary

HOLE	PAR	YARDS	EAGLES	BIRDIES	PARS	BOGEYS	D.BOGEYS	OTHER	RANK	AVERAGE
1	4	447	0	11	74	51	15	5	1	4.558
2	4	364	0	33	102	20	0	1	15	3.936
3	4	377	0	36	101	17	2	0	16	3.904
4	3	226	0	16	94	38	5	3	11	3.263
5	5	559	6	78	54	16	2	0	18	4.551
6	4	461	0	12	99	36	7	1	10	4.265
7	3	184	0	17	93	36	8	1	12	3.252
8	4	441	0	14	81	51	8	1	6	4.361
9	5	554	2	35	76	30	9	2	13	5.104
OUT	**36**	**3,613**	**8**	**252**	**774**	**295**	**56**	**14**		**37.162**
10	4	469	0	13	81	46	12	2	4	4.409
11	4	387	0	25	100	23	4	2	14	4.084
12	4	379	0	9	96	39	9	1	7	4.331
13	3	190	0	18	80	47	7	2	8	3.325
14	4	475	0	8	77	61	7	1	2	4.455
15	4	448	0	14	75	55	10	0	5	4.396
16	3	186	0	10	97	40	4	3	9	3.312
17	5	575	9	54	70	17	4	0	17	4.695
18	4	470	0	7	89	44	13	1	3	4.429
IN	**35**	**3,579**	**9**	**158**	**765**	**372**	**70**	**12**		**37.435**
TOTAL	**71**	**7,192**	**17**	**410**	**1539**	**667**	**126**	**26**		**74.597**

Garrick Porteous, the Amateur Champion, was on 76.

Spieth was playing with Matthew Fitzpatrick, at 18 the first Boys Amateur Champion to qualify since Sergio Garcia in 1998. He looked so fresh-faced that he was stopped for his badge on the practice range, but he can play. A double-bogey at the last stopped him from matching the 71 of 19-year-old Jimmy Mullen, an amateur from Royal North Devon.

Quite the shock of the day was McIlroy shooting a 79, during which he putted into a bunker at the 15th. The world number two claimed afterwards that he was "walking around out there and I'm unconscious. It's all mental." He had scored the same as Sir Nick Faldo, the double former winner at Muirfield, who celebrated his 56th birthday with a delightful sand escape from the bunker short of the 18th green.

Another of the home favourites, Luke Donald, crashed to an 80. Louis Oosthuizen, the 2010 Champion, had to withdraw with a neck injury after eight

Lee Westwood (72) headed out alongside Charl Schwartzel (75).

Rory McIlroy struggled to a 79.

holes, leaving Woods and Graeme McDowell as a twosome, while his compatriot Charl Schwartzel had an adventurous round. Schwartzel's drive at the ninth hit the out-of-bounds wall and bounded back to the fairway and he holed a bunker shot at the last, but on the 15th it all got a bit much for him when he hit a 6-iron from the rough less than perfectly and slammed the club into the ground in dejection. The ground was so hard that the club split in two, one end narrowly avoiding playing partner Sergio Garcia.

After that it was left for Kapur to make a late run up the leaderboard. The 31-year-old from New Delhi was out in the fourth-to-last group but raced to the turn in 30, birdieing six of the first seven holes (parring the short fourth). A double-bogey at the 10th stalled his progress, but he only dropped one more shot as the shadows lengthened. "It was the dream start," he said. "They were probably the fastest greens I've ever played in my life. They weren't green, they were white. That front nine was very special. I was in a bit of a trance. I was just trying to get as far under par as I could and then hold onto your hat coming in."

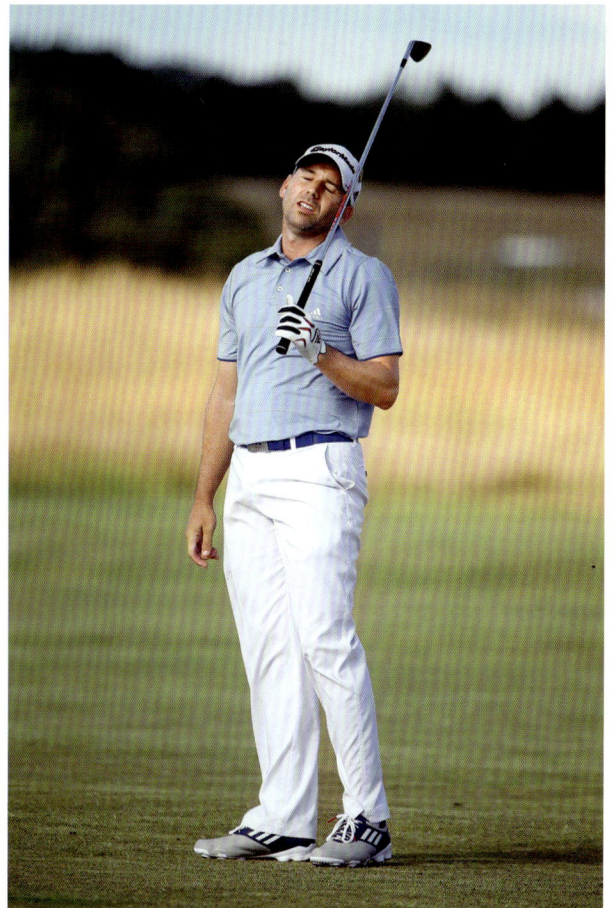
Not everything went according to plan in Sergio Garcia's 75.

FALDO ENJOYS A FINAL MUIRFIELD WALK

By Alistair Tait

Sir Nick Faldo wouldn't have been happy shooting 79 in his prime, but he was a contented man when he left Muirfield's 18th green after opening the 142nd Open Championship with that score. Faldo was back where he belonged, even if he couldn't live up to his halcyon days.

The three-time Open Champion was in one of the marquee groups on the opening day. He stepped onto the first tee alongside fellow seniors Tom Watson (right, with Faldo) and Fred Couples hoping to roll back the years one more time. He'd just turned 56 that morning and was hoping Muirfield would provide him with a nice birthday present.

Faldo began his love affair with The Open Championship at Muirfield. The home of the Honourable Company of Edinburgh Golfers was the scene of his first Open triumph, when he famously compiled 18 straight pars in the final round of the 1987 Championship to better Paul Azinger and Rodger Davis by a shot.

Open success followed in the 1990 Open at St Andrews before he tamed Muirfield again in 1992 to win his third Claret Jug. No wonder the Muirfield links tempted him out of retirement to play in the 142nd version of the game's oldest Major.

Faldo's previous Open appearance was thought to have been his last. He played in the 2010 Open Championship at St Andrews and missed the cut with scores of 72 and 81. That experience prompted him to retire from competitive golf to focus on off-course endeavours, including his Faldo Junior Series, course design and commentary work.

Faldo's time on the fairways wasn't exactly extensive following the 2010 Open Championship. He totalled just 35 rounds played in 2011 and 2012. The six-time Major winner was content with his life away from the fairways until he took a trip down memory lane.

"I was doing a commercial for Glenmorangie, and the question was, what's your favourite golf course," Faldo explained. "I thought, wow, I've got a very special place here, the 18th green at Muirfield. So maybe that sowed some seeds.

"About two months ago I was in my gym and I thought 'you're strong enough to have a go.' It might be the last chance I get to walk with fellow Open Champions. And so I said, 'okay, I'm going to go for it.'"

Recently, The Open Championship has conjured up some pretty amazing stories of former Champions nearly pulling off the impossible. Greg Norman came close at Royal Birkdale in 2008 at age 53, finishing third. A year later, five-time Open winner Watson lost to Stewart Cink in a playoff at Turnberry at age 59. Could Faldo emulate these two and somehow conjure up some of his old magic? The World Golf Hall of Famer was quick to dampen any hopes of pulling off the unexpected, especially after seeing the exacting test Muirfield posed for this Open Championship.

"When you've come and seen the test they've prepared, you start a grand idea of survival, of how close to the cut I could get," Faldo said. "That would be pretty impressive for a guy that hasn't hit a competitive shot for three years."

That statement was a far cry from the Faldo of old who turned up for most Majors in the late 1980s to mid 1990s expecting to contend. As you would expect from one of the most thorough of players during his heyday, Faldo poured everything into his preparation. However, two months wasn't enough time to eradicate three years of inactivity.

He bogeyed both of the first two holes and went to the turn in 38. Muirfield's tough inward nine then proved why bookmakers were right to discount Faldo's chances with odds of 1,000-1. Double-bogeys at the 14th and 17th holes along with dropped shots at the 13th and 16th saw the veteran limp home in 41 shots for a 79. He ended the day four shots worse than both his playing companions.

So how did the man known for his ultra competitiveness feel about breaking 80 in the opening round?

"I was enjoying it," he said, before adding, "I'm here to walk and enjoy. That's what I've got to remember."

There would be no grand comeback on day two from the greatest English golfer that ever lived. He did improve but not by much. He added a second-round 78 to miss the cut by six shots. Couples was the only one of the three who advanced to the weekend after scores of 75 and 74. Watson added a 78 to his opening 75.

It was a weary yet happy Faldo who met the press after his second round. The man who once delighted in taking on tough courses was honest enough to admit he didn't have it any more.

"It just wears you out," Faldo said. "I'm delighted I did it. I don't recommend it. Don't try something when you haven't practised, geez, don't do anything. Don't even go on the main roads unless you can turn the corner."

Despite the misery of not even coming close to his glory days, the Englishman derived an almost masochistic joy at being back between the ropes rather than commentating from outside them.

"It's a grinding fun. The whole experience was great. I've loved it. I came up here Sunday morning, like the good old days, as if I was trying to win, played lots of practice rounds. I played with Ernie (Els), played with Rosie (Justin Rose), (Henrik) Stenson, so that was fun. And I was able to try my best, which is cool."

As for the future, Faldo was ambivalent. "This is where it started with The Open. Maybe this is the right place to end it." Then in the very next breath he seemed to hint that 2015 at St Andrews might be where he really sees his Open career coming to an end. Maybe the idea of the iconic goodbye on the Swilcan Bridge is too good to pass up.

"Who knows? It's slim. At least I have that opportunity. So I will review it."

Faldo fans can live in hope for at least another two years anyway.

Close, and a Cigar

By Andy Farrell

Miguel Angel Jimenez takes the lead at three under par on the second day of The Open, but Westwood and Woods are lurking one behind.

The "breaking news" from the course on Friday morning of the 142nd Open Championship was that there were one or two ball marks to be repaired. Not many, and only on the first few greens for the very earliest of starters. But it was a nice line with which Lee Westwood and Tiger Woods could raise a laugh in their post-round interviews. Westwood and Woods were among those happy to have completed the first 36 holes of the Championship by lunchtime knowing that their positions were only going to improve in the afternoon.

Although the greens were hand-watered overnight, and some of the early starters were able to take advantage of greens that were marginally more holding, by the end of the day the scoring was higher than for the first round by almost a full stroke. The speed of the greens did not change as abruptly as the previous day, but they were still mighty quick. The temperature was not quite as warm as Thursday, but it was another day when the East Lothian coast resembled a Mediterranean idyll. The big difference, however, was that the wind switched by 180 degrees to come out of the east.

For those who had only got to play practice rounds since Monday, such as first-round leader Zach Johnson, it was a direction they had not yet experienced. It may have only been a 12mph zephyr, but players had to adapt to a course that now had three of the four short holes playing into the wind and holes such as the 14th and 15th playing downwind. They might have played shorter — amateur Ben Stow drove the green at the 448-yard 15th — but that did not make them easier. The 15th hole, which was the fifth hardest on Thursday, now became the hardest of all.

Where there had been 20 players under par in the first round, only nine remained in red figures

Miguel Angel Jimenez added a 71 to be the halfway leader.

Henrik Stenson was the first player to post two under par, which only Jimenez could better.

Low Scores

Low First Nine

Lee Westwood	31

Low Second Nine

Sandy Lyle	33
Graham DeLaet	33
Alvaro Quiros	33
Scott Jamieson	33

Low Round

Lee Westwood	68
Charl Schwartzel	68

after day two. In comparison to 14 sub-70 figures on Thursday, Friday saw only four. Westwood and Charl Schwartzel, who were playing together, both scored three-under-par 68s, which took the South African to one over par and the Englishman to two under. Henrik Stenson was the first player to finish at two under, after a second successive 70, and when Westwood and Woods, who had a 71, joined the Swede there were still four players ahead of them who were either on the course or yet to tee-off.

By the end of the day, only Miguel Angel Jimenez, who added a 71 to his earlier 68, had bettered their total at three under par. "I have to say the golf course is in very good shape," Jimenez said, "but to me it is extremely hard. With the wind, some pin positions, the ball cannot stay. It is a little bit too hard for me."

Yet, the engaging 49-year-old cigar-smoking Spaniard was leading The Open and able to look down on the rest. Dustin Johnson made it a fourball at two under par, but Zach Johnson fell back to one under, as did Rafael Cabrera-Bello, with Angel Cabrera and Scotland's Martin Laird finishing on the same mark.

Zach Johnson took a drop on the 18th hole as he finished with a bogey.

Dustin Johnson bogeyed the eighth hole but finished at two under par.

"Chomping on a cigar, the ponytailed Miguel Angel Jimenez strolled down the Muirfield range wearing aviator sunglasses, clutching a bottle of his beloved red Rioja wine. His beautiful blond girlfriend followed. 'Maybe the coolest man alive,' Keegan Bradley marvelled in a tweet."

—**Robert Lusetich, Fox Sports**

"Certainly, Westwood is at ease with himself. And why wouldn't he be, given the way the week has gone?"

—**Kevin Garside, *The Independent***

"You may notice something peculiar about the leaderboard: no talented young whippersnappers in the lot. Jimenez is 49, Westwood is 40. Woods and Stenson, aka the Iceman, are 37. Dustin Johnson is 29, but an experienced 29 with seven PGA Tour victories and lots of experience contending in the Majors. … The average age of those tied at one under par is 35."

—**John Paul Newport, *Wall Street Journal***

"Andy Murray wins Wimbledon. St Johnstone beat Rosenborg away. The sun is shining. It's all wonderfully weird, isn't it? Well, Martin Laird believes he might just top off Scotland's scorching summer of sport by adding the Claret Jug to the country's trophy cabinet."

—**David McCarthy, *Daily Record***

Three birdies in a row on the inward nine helped Martin Laird to one under par.

Jordan Spieth dropped four shots on the last four holes.

Ryan Moore was at level par for 36 holes and an interesting pack of players at one over included 19-year-old Jordan Spieth, after dropping four strokes in the last four holes, the 2011 Champion Darren Clarke, despite an 8 at the sixth hole, Ian Poulter, who managed the rare feat of parring the entire second nine, and the last four Masters Champions, Adam Scott, Bubba Watson, Schwartzel and Phil Mickelson. In fact, the winners of 11 of the last 13 Masters were on the leaderboard at Muirfield.

Westwood might have been among their number had it not been for the brilliance of Mickelson in 2010. That was one of seven times the Englishman had finished in the top three of a Major Championship, but the now 40-year-old had put himself in position to try again to claim that elusive title.

Lee Westwood went out in 31 on the way to a 68.

Second Round Leaders

HOLE	1	2	3	4	5	6	7	8	9	10	11	12	13	14	15	16	17	18	
PAR	4	4	4	3	5	4	3	4	5	4	4	4	3	4	4	3	5	4	TOTAL
Miguel Angel Jimenez	4	(3)	4	[4]	5	4	3	4	5	4	(3)	4	3	[5]	4	3	5	4	71-139
Henrik Stenson	(3)	4	4	3	5	[6]	(2)	4	(4)	[5]	(3)	4	3	4	[5]	3	(4)	4	70-140
Lee Westwood	(3)	(3)	4	3	(4)	4	3	(3)	(4)	4	4	(3)	[4]	[5]	4	3	5	[5]	68-140
Tiger Woods	4	4	(3)	[4]	(4)	4	3	[5]	5	4	[5]	4	3	4	4	3	5	(3)	71-140
Dustin Johnson	[5]	4	4	[4]	(3)	[5]	3	[5]	(4)	4	4	(3)	3	4	[5]	3	5	4	72-140

Justin Leonard, the 1997 Champion, posted 70 to be two over.

Darren Clarke returned a 71 despite an 8 at the sixth hole.

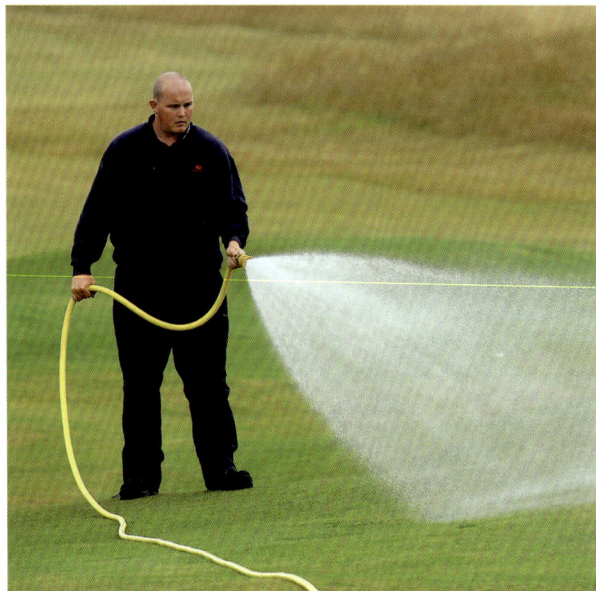

The greens were hand-watered overnight.

While world number two Rory McIlroy, US Open Champion Justin Rose and Luke Donald all headed home after missing the cut, and Paul Lawrie, the last Briton to win The Open in 1999, went home and then came back again when the cut-line rose late in the day, Westwood was relaxing in his temporary home next to the Muirfield clubhouse. "I'll kick back this afternoon on the couch and watch the struggles, and the cricket," he said, referring to the coverage of his fellow competitors as well as the Ashes Test match at Lord's in which England were hammering the Australians. No doubt his son, Sam, who had followed his father every step of the round, would have preferred to keep repeating the highlights of his dad's play.

There were plenty from which to choose. He

Spain's Rafael Cabrera-Bello dropped back with a 74.

holed from 20 feet at the first and 18 feet at the second before getting up and down from a green-side bunker for a 4 at the par-5 fifth, where he had played a driver from the deck for his second shot now that the hole was playing into the wind. He ended the first nine by holing from 15 feet at the eighth and making a 4 at the ninth to be out in 31, the best half of the day.

His friend Clarke also had a good first nine going when he birdied three holes in a row from the third but he then got into trouble at the sixth. Driving into thick rough, he played safe for his second but put his third into a bunker and was plugged under the lip. He took three swings to escape and then two-putted for a quadruple-bogey. "I was running out of fingers counting how many I'd taken," said

Angel Cabrera challenged for the lead but finished one under.

Adam Scott was among those on one over as he sought the Claret Jug that eluded him in 2012.

Second Round Scores	
Players Under Par	11
Players At Par	15
Players Over Par	127

the Northern Irishman, who has not always been so phlegmatic about his misfortunes on the course.

Clarke steadied his ship for a 71, but it showed that disaster lurked at every turn. Westwood, however, went on his way and birdied the 12th with a wedge approach to two feet to get to six under for the day and tied for the lead at five under with the yet-to-tee-off Zach Johnson. From there on, he drifted back again only to regain most of the ground once his round was over. He three-putted the 13th, got out of position off the tee at the 14th and found a bunker by the final green to drop three strokes.

"It's not easy out there," he said. "I think a 68 is a good round. I was playing some great stuff and it was just getting harder as the holes progressed, tougher to score, tougher to get it close. To be two under is a real bonus, it could be leading at the end of the day, you never know."

He added: "I love playing in The Open Championship. This is the biggest tournament of the year for me, being a Brit and it being played in Britain. Why not enjoy it out there? It's tough for everybody, so smile your way through."

Westwood and his family moved to Florida over the winter. The new life has suited the entire family but being based at Old Palm in

Charl Schwartzel matched Westwood's 68 for the best score of the day.

North Palm Beach has certainly helped Westwood's golf. His short game saw swift improvement and he had recently started working with Sean Foley, coach to Woods and Rose, on the swing and had got some tips on the greens from Ian Baker-Finch, whose silky putting skills brought the Australian an Open title in 1991. "I got a couple of tips on getting tension out of my arms and having a bit more control," Westwood explained. "I'm getting it on-line nicely and I've gauged the pace of the greens well."

"Lee definitely surprised me," said Schwartzel. "I thought he putted beautifully. The putts he needed to make, he has made. That's been the difference with him so far this week. He's made a whole bunch of par putts that keep the momentum going. He's a dangerman."

Schwartzel had an interesting round himself, with just one bogey and four birdies, the first of which came when he drove pin-high left of the second green, in the gully between the green and the out-of-bounds wall. Admitting he was not proud of having snapped a club in anger the previous day, he revealed his mannerism of placing his left hand in his pocket while lining up a putt was to do with releasing tension from his shoulders.

If there was an ominous putt holed on the 18th green on Friday morning it was a 15-footer by Woods that brought a flourish of the

Round of the Day: **Lee Westwood - 68**

OFFICIAL SCORECARD
THE OPEN CHAMPIONSHIP 2013
MUIRFIELD

Lee WESTWOOD
Game 14
Friday 19 July at 9:00am ✓

FOR R&A USE ONLY [k]		ROUND 2
18 HOLE TOTAL	72	36 HOLE TOTAL
THIS ROUND	68	
36 HOLE TOTAL	140	140 .

VERIFIED **I GD**

ROUND 2

Hole	1	2	3	4	5	6	7	8	9	Out	10	11	12	13	14	15	16	17	18	In	Total
Yards	447	364	377	226	559	461	184	441	554	3613	469	387	379	190	475	448	186	575	470	3579	7192
Par	4	4	4	3	5	4	3	4	5	36	4	4	4	3	4	4	3	5	4	35	71
Score	3	3	4	3	4	4	3	3	4	31	4	4	3	4	5	4	3	5	5	37	68

Signature of Marker

Signature of Competitor
Lee Westwood

Noteworthy

- **Hole 1:** 3-iron, 9-iron, one putt from 20 feet
- **Hole 2:** 4-iron, wedge, one putt from 18 feet
- **Hole 5:** Driver, driver, sand wedge from greenside bunker, one putt from eight feet
- **Hole 8:** 2-iron, 5-iron, one putt from 15 feet
- **Hole 9:** Fairway wood, 5-iron, two putts from short of green, 45 feet, holing from six feet
- **Hole 12:** 7-iron, wedge, one putt from two feet
- **Hole 13:** Three putts
- **Hole 14:** Driver right rough, chip out, lob wedge, two putts from 35 feet
- **Hole 18:** 3-wood, 7-iron, sand wedge from greenside bunker, two putts from eight feet

Graeme McDowell helped out at the MasterCard bar.

putter and a brief fist pump. The birdie brought the world number one back to level par for the day and right in contention once again. A conservative strategy meant he had not yet used his driver in two days, but his 57 putts for 36 holes was only bettered by the 55 of Westwood, Schwartzel and Jimenez. "I'm in a good spot," Woods said. "I'm just going to continue plodding along, being patient, putting the ball in the right spots. We're not going to get a lot of opportunities out there, but when I have, I've been able to capitalise and hopefully that will continue."

Confirmation of the theory that Woods was perfectly poised to strike for his first Major victory in five years came from his playing partner, Graeme McDowell — they were a twoball after the withdrawal of Louis Oosthuizen the previous day. "He was very impressive the last two days," McDowell said. "He will not be far away. He plays the course

Tiger Woods looked in ominous form as he holed for birdie on the 18th green.

"They say every cloud has a silver lining. Mine is that I will be able to attend my sister Samantha's wedding near Dollar today. I always intended to be at the evening reception but crashing out of The Open yesterday means I'll be present for the official part as well."

—**Scott Jamieson,
player diary,** *The Sun*

"Rarely has Westwood putted better. Most impressive for a player that has often wielded his putter with all the subtlety of a sledgehammer was that he had 18 single putts, many from about 12 feet, over the first 36 holes."

—**Peter Dixon,** *The Times*

"Even the greats can be grinders. Tiger Woods, unpicking Muirfield's defences with the dexterity of a neurosurgeon, is carving a path towards a 15th Major Championship coronation as if he is wielding not a cavity-back 3-iron but a scalpel."

—**Oliver Brown,** *The Daily Telegraph*

"What's going to happen to Mr Unlucky this time? Will Tiger Woods bounce his second shot off a sprinkler head into the hole on the 18th to beat him by one? Perhaps 56-year-old Mark O'Meara will shoot the first 62 in Major Championship history to pip him on the line? After all, Lee Westwood can't win The Open, can he? Something always happens."

—**Derek Lawrenson,** *Daily Mail*

2

Miguel Angel Jimenez
Happy in His Own Skin

Considering that he had broken his left leg in a skiing accident in December and been in plaster for four months, that his leg had not fully recovered its strength and that he was suffering from tennis elbow, Miguel Angel Jimenez, by rights, should not have been anywhere near the leaderboard after 36 holes, never mind on top of it. On a shorter, less demanding course he might have been, perhaps, but not one as bone-hard and stomach-wrenchingly difficult as Muirfield.

But there's the rub with Jimenez. Precious little is conventional about the Spaniard, from the length of his hair, to the gymnastic routine he goes through to warm up; from the snakeskin shoes he has made for himself to the huge cigars he smokes. From top to toe, Jimenez is a one-off.

Yet there he was on Friday night three under par and leading by one stroke after rounds of 68 and a two-birdie and two-bogey 71, level par. His birdies in the second round had come neatly and symmetrically at the second and 11th thanks to a four-foot putt and one of 15 feet. He dropped shots on the fourth and 14th as a result of missing the green on each hole with his approach with a 3-iron.

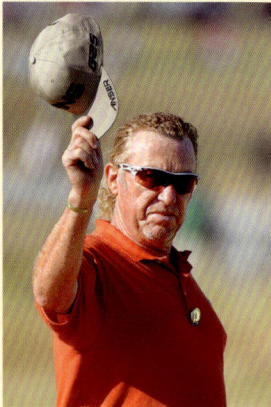

Jimenez, 49, was attempting to become the oldest winner of a Major Championship, and Rafael Cabrera-Bello, his young countryman, was two strokes behind. Jimenez's secret? Do what makes him happy and not what others do or what might make others happy. The French have a phrase for it: *heureux dans votre proper peau*, meaning happy in your own skin. Jimenez certainly is.

Asked how he was leading The Open at his age, he affected mock indignation, widening his eyes, raising his eyebrows and saying: "Why? I have not the right to do it? Only the young people can do it?" When the laughter subsided, he continued: "I've been 25 years on tour, had 19 victories and I would love to have a Major, so why not this one? The secret is to enjoy what you do in life. Have fun. That does not mean falling on the ground laughing. Having fun is what I am doing. I feel relaxed. I play golf for a living and have been doing the same thing for 25 years. I keep elastic and flexible. I'm still training and walking."

And still making us admire him as much for his attitude to life as for his undoubted golfing skills.

—John Hopkins

Webb Simpson scored 70 to be one over par.

very conservatively, but it is incredible how well he controls his ball flight. He is using his iron play to devastating effect, and combined with some great putting, he's going to be dangerous. I said to him on 18, 'That was a clinic the last two days.'"

McDowell, the 2010 US Open Champion, added: "It's nice to be the only man in that twoball with a Major in the last five years, but you can fall into the trap of standing back and admiring what is happening beside you. I'm looking forward to getting into my own zone tomorrow. It wouldn't surprise me if he's picking up the Claret Jug on Sunday night, but I'm not writing off the rest of the field, and certainly not myself."

Why would he when the Northern Irishman had the power of binary golf on his side. By some strange decree, McDowell was either putting up 0s

Ian Poulter, who parred the entire inward nine, plays from a bunker at the 18th hole.

or 1s — since April he had either missed the cut, as he had done five times including at the Masters and the US Open, or won, as he did at the Heritage on the PGA Tour, and at the Volvo World Match Play and the Alstom French Open, his last outing. By making the cut at four over par after a 71, surely there was no other winner? "Get your money on me now," he laughed. "I only win when I make cuts, apparently.

"I certainly didn't want to be sitting at home watching this on TV," he said. "I'm ecstatic to be here, it's going to be a beautiful weekend. The golf course is going to get nothing but tougher and tougher. It is tough to see the leaders getting beyond four or five under. Literally anything under par could win. We saw how difficult it became yesterday. After today, I'd imagine they can let the hand brake off and let the course accelerate away from us."

There were few complaints about the setup of the course for the second round, but the trickiest pin position was undoubtedly at the 15th, where the hole was in the back right quadrant, protected by the famous ridge that runs through the green. Brandt Snedeker four-putted, lipping out twice, on the way to an inward 43 and a round of 79. He still made the cut, but Nicolas Colsaerts went home after a 9 at the 15th which included five putts, most of them misguided attempts at ramming the ball in the hole.

Poulter, who was critical of some of the pin positions in the first

In the Words of the Competitors…

"

"I'm up here and playing in a big tournament again. I think I've got the experience to do well in these Championships. Tough conditions is something I enjoy and suits my game."

—Henrik Stenson

"I played some flawless golf around the front nine, and I got a little out of position on the back nine. And I really managed to hang in there."

—Ian Poulter

"We're not going to get a lot of opportunities out there, but when I have, I've been able to capitalise, and, hopefully, I can continue doing that."

—Tiger Woods

"I probably have higher expectations for myself than everyone in the crowd. It's not something I'm really worried about. You can only look at it as something that can help you. They can pull you along."

—Martin Laird

"I love links golf. And I'm trying to be as positive as I can. For some reason, I guess I got all my breaks last year. I'm not getting anything, and it's very frustrating, trying to get myself back in the tournament."

—Ernie Els

"

Excerpts FROM THE Press

"Fun is not a word that has been bandied around much by the players at Muirfield this week, but Jordan Spieth, the youngest winner on the PGA Tour in more than 80 years, is having the time of his life."

—**James Riach,** *The Guardian*

"Darren Clarke kept his head on after a nightmare quadruple-bogey-8 threatened to wreck his chances of another Open win. After taking three shots to escape after plugging his third shot under the lip of a greenside bunker at the sixth, he resisted the temptation to lose his cool and signed for a 71 that left him four shots off the lead on one over par."

—**Brian Keogh,** *Irish Golf Desk*

"Only the strong-willed answer the call and, as he has proven in a professional career thrust upon him in near-fairy-tale fashion with his Irish Open win of 2009 when still an amateur, Shane Lowry possesses his fair share of fortitude. The boy has grown into a man."

—**Philip Reid,** *The Irish Times*

"Firm, fast and fiery Muirfield continues to resemble a yellow brick road. There will be a golfing wizard at the end of it, but who it will be remains to be seen."

—**Nick Rodger,** *The Herald*

American Hunter Mahan was well placed after two rounds of 72.

round, was not biting again. "I said enough yesterday," he said. "I two-putted 15 so I'm happy." Mickelson also got a par at the 15th, only to four-putt at the 16th for a double-bogey-5. "I missed a couple of short ones and that's going to happen to everyone. Fortunately, I made a heck of a lot more of my share today," he said.

Mickelson, who had two double-bogeys in his 74, added: "When I made those comments yesterday I was not being totally fair to The R&A. They've done a lot of things great this Championship. The setup is great. For me to single out a few sketchy pin placements and not give them credit for all the good things they've done was not fair of me.

"I think it is set up where, if you're playing well, you can make up ground and separate yourself. Really solidly struck shots are giving you easy pars and potential birdies. And poorly struck shots are making it extremely difficult to salvage par. So it's going to be a good test to be able to separate yourself if you're playing well."

Those not playing well included McIlroy, who had a 75 to be 12 over, Rose, who scored a 77 to be 10 over, and Donald, who improved to a 72, but the damage had been done the previous day and he was also at 10 over par. While the likes of Padraig Harrington and Sergio Garcia thought they might have missed the cut at six over, late in

56 • *The Open Championship 2013*

Round Two Hole Summary

HOLE	PAR	YARDS	EAGLES	BIRDIES	PARS	BOGEYS	D.BOGEYS	OTHER	RANK	AVERAGE
1	4	447	0	6	104	38	4	1	10	4.281
2	4	364	0	22	93	36	2	0	13	4.118
3	4	377	0	19	97	34	3	0	12	4.137
4	3	226	0	8	85	51	9	0	6	3.399
5	5	559	1	38	82	27	5	0	16	4.980
6	4	461	0	3	78	62	8	2	2	4.536
7	3	184	0	14	114	21	4	0	14	3.098
8	4	441	0	5	78	56	11	3	2	4.536
9	5	554	4	84	50	14	0	1	18	4.510
OUT	**36**	**3,613**	**5**	**199**	**781**	**339**	**46**	**7**		**37.595**
10	4	469	0	12	83	48	9	1	8	4.373
11	4	387	0	15	113	20	5	0	15	4.098
12	4	379	0	35	102	14	2	0	17	3.889
13	3	190	0	12	89	42	9	1	9	3.333
14	4	475	0	7	77	61	6	2	5	4.477
15	4	448	1	10	61	66	12	3	1	4.582
16	3	186	0	8	86	52	5	2	7	3.392
17	5	575	0	22	92	33	6	0	11	5.150
18	4	470	0	13	70	57	9	4	4	4.484
IN	**35**	**3,579**	**1**	**134**	**773**	**393**	**63**	**13**		**37.778**
TOTAL	**71**	**7,192**	**6**	**333**	**1554**	**732**	**109**	**20**		**75.373**

the day the cut actually went to eight over with 84 players qualifying for the weekend. It would have been 70 at seven over had Camilo Villegas had a par at the last instead of a double-bogey which took him to nine over.

Lawrie had driven home to Aberdeen after a terrific 69 in the morning had only got him back to eight over. He re-gripped some new clubs in his garage, took his West Highland terrier, Bobo, for a walk and had some dinner before realising he and wife Marian ought to drive the two and a half hours back to Muirfield, where his room at the Greywalls Hotel, next to the clubhouse, was awaiting him. He had had to pay for a seven-night minimum stay regardless. Thongchai Jaidee had flown down to Heathrow, and was awaiting a connection for Bangkok, when he too realised he needed to be flying back to Edinburgh instead.

Zach Johnson, whose par putt at the first hovered

Phil Mickelson was feeling positive despite a 74.

Tom Lehman, like fellow Champion Mark O'Meara, started in red figures but returned a 77 on Friday.

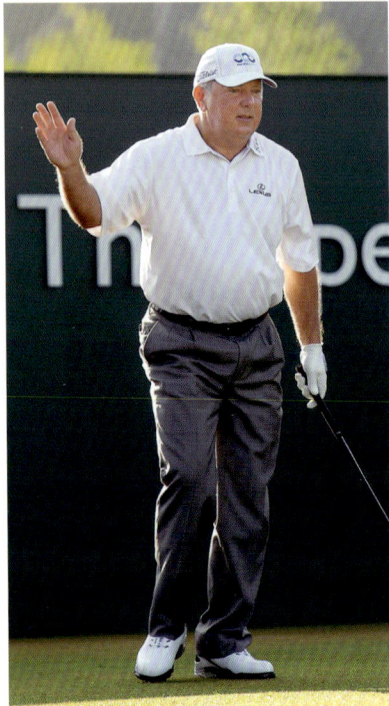

Mark O'Meara limped back with a 78.

Japan's Hideki Matsuyama was two over.

Justin Rose missed the cut after a 77.

Unlike playing partners Sir Nick Faldo and Tom Watson, Fred Couples safely qualified for the weekend.

on the edge defying gravity and later three-putted the 15th for a double-bogey, was still leading at five under with five holes to play but dropped four shots in that time. "There weren't that many bad shots," said the 2007 Masters winner. "It was a grind right from the first until that four-footer at the last."

Cabrera had been contesting the lead with the American but dropped three shots in his last five holes, so it was Jimenez, after just two birdies and only two bogeys, who inherited the halfway lead. Rather cheekily, he was asked: "How are you leading The Open at 49 years old?" Jimenez replied: "Why? I have not the right to do it? Only the young people can do it?"

He added: "I don't know what's going to happen on Sunday afternoon. I don't know what is going to happen tomorrow. I'm going to hit some balls now. My coach is waiting. And I'm going to have a nice cigar and some nice wine. And when tomorrow is coming, when the sun is coming, I will deal with that thing." As Jimenez left his favourite restaurant in North Berwick that evening, the leader of The Open Championship received a standing ovation from his fellow diners.

It's a Fact

Kyle Stanley improved by 13 strokes between his first round of 82 and second round of 69, while Scott Piercy's 88 was 14 strokes worse than his first round of 74. The greatest improvement from one round to another in The Open was the 22 strokes (94-72) by Robin Davenport at Muirfield in 1966. Colin Montgomerie shares the record for the greatest increase in score (20 strokes) with his 64 followed by 84 at Muirfield in 2002.

A HUMBLING EXPERIENCE

By Lewine Mair

In the opinion of Tom Lehman, the pressures of playing in front of a home crowd are tougher on this side of the Atlantic than they are in the US. When the 1996 Champion was asked why Europeans were not featuring to the same degree as Americans, he said he could sense the greater weight of expectation on UK players.

"The expectation is something that can work for you or against you — and you can either embrace it and really feel the love and draw energy from the crowd or you feel that added pressure that doesn't allow you to perform," Lehman said. "And I think there's a lot of that at The Open — more so here than there is in the US Open."

Lehman cited Luke Donald (left), who had opened at Muirfield with an 80. "Look at Luke yesterday and the way he struggled," said Lehman, feelingly. "Expectations are so high and everybody is saying, 'This is a great course for Luke Donald.'"

There are years when people would have been saying the same of Rory McIlroy (above) or Justin Rose but this was a week when the well-organised Donald was seen as the player most likely to be able to marry his game to the slippery Open links. McIlroy was as a man in a Scottish haar, while Rose was still in recovery, if that is the right word, from winning the US Open.

It was entirely predictable that McIlroy's missed cut would receive more attention than those of his two Ryder Cup companions.

This two-time Major winner had a sad, and shocking, 79 to open and followed up with a 75 to miss the cut on the same number as Vijay Singh. The 75 represented an improvement but, as he said, "I needed to get off to a fast start to have any chance of being here for the weekend. When I was five over after seven, that wasn't going to happen," McIlroy said.

What hurt the Ulsterman most was that this was the first time he had missed the cut in The Open.

Typically, he lost no ground in terms of how he is perceived by the public. On the first day, spectators had been as a team coming together to push some recalcitrant car into action; they could not have poured more of themselves into bringing him back to life. On the second day, when they realised he was going nowhere in this Open, their encouragement turned to sympathy, though they happily shared in one lighter moment at the penultimate hole. As Rory finally made a birdie, so he gave a humorously cheeky little fist pump.

In his press conference, McIlroy said he could not be too disappointed with himself in that he had done "everything I could have done but it didn't work out." Looking for positives, he said he had hit his driver over the last few holes by way of practising for the WGC event at Akron and that he had hit it well.

He had already acknowledged that he needed to improve his schedule, though there were plenty to wonder what hope he had on that score whilst trying to make his schedule and Caroline Wozniacki's work hand in hand. With his previous girlfriend, Holly, the only dates he had to bear in mind were those attaching to Holly's school holidays.

"It's like life," considered McIlroy in surveying his career as a whole. "You're going to go through highs and you're going to go through lows. It's about trying to work your way out of the lows. Sooner or later, things will turn round and I'll play the golf that everyone knows that I'm capable of — and that's capable of winning Major Championships."

Donald and Rose pulled up on 10 over par as against McIlroy's 12 over. Donald had needed something a whole lot more spectacular than a 72 if he were to make up for that opening 80, while Rose's rounds of 75 and 77 told their own story of a man who had been run off his feet in the wake of his US Open. "I wasn't quite prepared to play again," he admitted. "My game never felt great coming in here. I thought I could get it back each day, but it was not to be."

His second round included two double-bogeys, one at the sixth and the other at the 10th, and two bogeys at the 11th and 18th.

"Golf humbles you and I have been humbled many times," said Rose who, when he turned professional, missed 21 successive cuts by way of a less than promising start to his 15-year path to a first Major.

To those who asked if his failure at Muirfield had anything to do with the pressure, Rose reminded his audience that it was more a matter of Majors being tough to win. "Guys spend their whole lives trying to win one, let alone two," he said.

Two other notables to miss the halfway cut, albeit only by a single shot, were Nicolas Colsaerts and Alvaro Quiros. Out on the practice range at the start of the week, both had sent balls soaring over the back netting at a time when others were arriving at that boundary via a couple of bounces.

When it came to The Open itself, the pair suffered all the frustrations of having only a handful of occasions when they could give rein to their enviably long hitting.

Mind you, it was not Colsaerts' driver that did him the greatest mischief over his lacklustre 75 and 76. It was his putter. When he came to the 15th in his second round, he had a horror of a five-putt 9 which was not the kind of on-course calamity that the others professionals wanted to hear about.

Muirfield in its 2013 guise was no place for anything less than 100 percent positive thoughts.

Third Round

Westwood Ho!

By Andy Farrell

Lee Westwood takes a two-stroke lead after 54 holes to give himself another chance of winning the title he wants most, The Open Championship.

For very good reasons, the penultimate pairing of the penultimate round of the 142nd Open Championship felt as if it was the final group of the final day. Lee Westwood and Tiger Woods are no strangers to each other. Their careers have coincided and for most of that time one has been the best player from his nation and the other the best player in the world. Despite the disparity in Major titles (0-14), their mutual respect is total and forged in meetings in the Ryder Cup, Major Championships and on tour, where Westwood is one of the few ever to beat Woods when he was leading after 54 holes of a tournament at the Deutsche Bank Open in Hamburg in 2000.

Lee Westwood opened up a two-stroke lead with a 70.

From the moment they teed-off at 3.10pm there was an electric atmosphere as they toured Muirfield in this third round. By the time they walked up the 18th fairway in early evening to a rapturous ovation from the packed grandstands, it was Westwood who had edged in front with a 70 to the 72 of Woods.

As much as the pair commanded the attention of the gallery, it was hardly a match-play encounter. But the two shots that Westwood, at three under par, had gained over Woods was also his lead in the Championship, with Hunter Mahan joining Woods at one under. They were the only three players to remain under par. Adam Scott, a year on from his doomed quest for the Claret Jug at Royal Lytham, was at level par, with Henrik Stenson, Ryan Moore, Angel Cabrera and Zach Johnson at one over. How far was too far back? Phil Mickelson was alongside Francesco Molinari at two over par, Miguel Angel Jimenez, the 36-hole leader, had crashed back to three over and Ian Poulter was at five over.

In a bright orange shirt, only marginally less garish than the lime green–shocking yellow eye-blinder that he wore on the first day, Westwood

Excerpts
FROM THE Press

"This was Lee Westwood's day and now the world will tune in to see if it is, at last, his moment. What a tale this would be, if Westwood could emulate his great friend, Darren Clarke, and win The Open in his 40s."

—James Corrigan,
The Sunday Telegraph

"After his disappointing fade down the stretch of the US Open, Hunter Mahan guaranteed he'd be ready the next time in the final pair on the last day of a Major. He won't have to wait long to prove it. The Texan left The Open late Saturday afternoon as one of only three golfers with a red number alongside his name."

—Jim Litke, The Associated Press

"Japan's Hideki Matsuyama was hit by a one-stroke penalty for slow play during the third round of The Open Championship on Saturday, the second player this year assessed such a penalty in a Major. … The Royal & Ancient said before the tournament it would be more strict about enforcing slow-play guidelines and expected twoball games to play in 3 hours, 41 minutes. … At the Masters this year, 14-year-old Guan Tianlang was penalised one shot."

—Bob Harig, ESPN.com

"Twenty-one painful, protracted minutes. That's how long it took for Martin Laird to play his way out of Open Championship contention."

—Alan Campbell, *The Sunday Times*

Hunter Mahan matched the best score of the day with a 68.

stood out for more reasons than one. His duel with Woods swung one way, then the other. Early on he went three ahead, only to be caught again by Woods a few holes later. He edged ahead by one at the 14th, but dropped a shot at the 16th. It was the 17th which decided the honours for the day, Westwood playing the par 5 conventionally and holing from 15 feet for a birdie but Woods making the cardinal error of finding the cross bunkers for his second shot and taking a bogey-6.

Once again it was his putting that gave Westwood a reassuring air of a player on the verge of breaking his Major duck. Too often while compiling his seven top-three finishes in Grand Slam events, it had been his putting that proved the weak link. No more. Refreshed by a tip from former Open Champion Ian Baker-Finch, Westwood was holing out with confidence. There was the flashy 45-footer he holed from short of the fifth green for an eagle, but the really significant development was the way he holed the ones that mattered down the stretch. After he raced his first putt at the 15th six feet past, he made

Adam Scott moved within three of the lead.

Third Round Leaders

HOLE	1	2	3	4	5	6	7	8	9	10	11	12	13	14	15	16	17	18	TOTAL
PAR	4	4	4	3	5	4	3	4	5	4	4	4	3	4	4	3	5	4	TOTAL
Lee Westwood	4	4	[5]	3	(3)	4	(2)	5	[6]	4	4	4	3	(3)	4	[4]	(4)	4	70-210
Hunter Mahan	(3)	(3)	4	[4]	5	4	3	4	(4)	4	4	4	[4]	4	(3)	3	(4)	4	68-212
Tiger Woods	4	(3)	4	[4]	5	4	[4]	4	(4)	4	4	3	4	4	3	[6]	4	4	72-212
Adam Scott	4	4	(3)	[4]	5	4	3	4	(4)	[5]	4	4	(2)	4	4	3	5	4	70-213

Low Scores

Low First Nine

Hunter Mahan	34
Sergio Garcia	34
Brandt Snedeker	34
Shingo Katayama	34
Keegan Bradley	34
Thomas Bjorn	34
Matt Kuchar	34
Todd Hamilton	34

Low Second Nine

Geoff Ogilvy	32

Low Round

Hunter Mahan	68
Sergio Garcia	68
Richard Sterne	68

America's Ryan Moore was tied for fifth after a 72.

the one back for par. After missing the green in an awful spot at the 16th, he turned a double-bogey into a bogey by holing from 20 feet. And with Woods in trouble at the 17th, he converted his own birdie chance to open up some welcome daylight between him and the rest.

"Those are the sort of things you need to do and the sort of things that have been missing, making that putt at 16 and then backing it up with the birdie at the next hole," he said. Having only taken 81 putts in the first three rounds, five fewer than anyone else, Westwood was doing to the field what Woods usually does. "I figured if I'm going to win this tournament, I was going to have to beat Tiger," he added.

"It generally works like that, whatever tournament he's playing in. That wasn't my primary goal going out, it was just to get as many birdies as possible and to get as far in front as I could. But I have a good relationship with Tiger and I enjoy playing with him. I tend to feed off how good a player he is. I think my recent record playing with him in Major Championships is very good."

While Woods continued to plot his way around the course and had not by any stretch played his way out of contention, his inability

Tiger Woods at the 13th tee before falling two behind Westwood with a 72.

Adam Scott
Trying to Banish Demons From 2012

Adam Scott arrived at this year's Open Championship with more to prove than most. Only a win would eradicate the pain of 12 months earlier.

Scott bogeyed the last four holes at Royal Lytham in 2012 to lose the title to Ernie Els. His Masters victory in April helped ease that pain. However, the Australian turned up at Muirfield hoping to make amends for his failure the year before.

"This really has been the tournament I've been looking forward to most this year, there's no doubt, for obvious reasons," Scott said on the eve of the Championship. "After what happened at Lytham, I was eager to get back and try and get into another position to hopefully win the Claret Jug."

Scott found himself in a good position after 36 holes, returning rounds of 71 and 72 to lie just four shots off Miguel Angel Jimenez's lead. A good third round and he'd be just where he wanted to be.

The Australian set off on Open Saturday in the company of fellow Masters winner Charl Schwartzel. Scott proved a model of consistency, outscoring his South African playing companion by six shots. Scott returned a one-under-par 70 on a day that proved tough for scoring. Only 12 players broke par, and the average score for the field was 73.89.

Scott went out in 35, one under par, with birdies at the third and ninth holes, and a bogey at the fourth. He bogeyed the 10th to fall back to level par, but picked up a shot on the par-3 13th to be one under for the day.

"It was a good round of golf today," Scott said. "I hit a lot of really good shots. It was really solid stuff. I made a couple of putts. Made a couple of mistakes, but I think overall one under par out there today is a really solid round of golf. It puts me in good position for tomorrow."

Scott had attained the goal he had set himself at the start of the week. He was in contention to win the Championship. The question was: would he banish the demons that haunted him a year earlier?

We know the answer to that question. Scott experienced a strange sense of déjà vu in the final round. Once again he took the lead only to run up four bogeys and watch someone else tear the Claret Jug from his grasp. Still, he managed to take the positives from another strong performance in The Open Championship.

"I like where my game's at," Scott said after finishing in a tie for third. "I was contending most of the week. That's where I want to be. That's where I've got to keep myself. And, yeah, I believe I can win another one soon."

Perhaps as soon as the 143rd Open Championship at Royal Liverpool next year. Scott is sure to be a favourite when the world's best gather at England's second oldest links. Maybe by then he will have figured out how to win the Claret Jug.

—**Alistair Tait**

Henrik Stenson faltered with a 74 to drop four strokes off the lead.

to press ahead on the weekend of Majors in recent times remained puzzling. Not since the final round of the Masters in 2011 had he scored in the 60s on the weekend of a Major and nor had he done so in The Open since the third round at Carnoustie in 2007, the year after he collected the third of his Claret Jugs. "Lee played solid and made a couple of big putts at 16 and 17," Woods said.

"I was trying to grind along and play my own game, regardless of what Lee or anyone else was doing. This course is a tough test and I felt I played well. I'm pleased where I'm at, only two back and there's only one guy ahead of me."

Woods was showing no sign of the elbow injury that hampered his efforts at the US Open at Merion, but not having played in competition since then perhaps meant his game was not as sharp as he would like. It was five years since the last of his 14 Major wins and, famously, he had never won a Major without leading or sharing the lead after 54 holes.

"I've got 14 of these things and I know what it takes to win," he said. "Lee's won tournaments all over the world and knows what

Third Round Scores	
Players Under Par	12
Players At Par	5
Players Over Par	67

Brandt Snedeker's 69 was 10 better than the day before.

Zach Johnson stayed in contention despite the frustration.

it takes to win. He's two ahead but it's not just the two of us. There's a bunch of guys who have a chance to win this tournament. All of us really need to play well tomorrow. Hopefully, I can play a little better and make a couple more putts."

Westwood said: "Even though I have not won a Major, I know what it takes to win one. It's just a case of going out there and having confidence in my game, which I've got. It's enjoyable, it's where you want to be. It's great to play in an Open Championship in front of the crowds they have got here. I always get a good reception, but it's nice to play well and hear those roars."

Westwood's performance was also impressive for what was going on around him. In the final 10 pairings of the day, no one beat his score of 70 and only Scott, who teed-off five groups earlier, matched it. Half of those players failed to break 75. One of them was the overnight leader Jimenez, who had a 77. A shot went for the Spaniard at the second, but he played a marvellous bunker shot at

Former Champion Padraig Harrington's 77 was disappointing.

Jason Day stayed in contention with a 72.

Jamie Donaldson posted a second successive 71.

It's a
Fact

The one-stroke penalty for slow play charged to Hideki Matsuyama in the third round ultimately cost Matsuyama a qualification for the 2014 Masters Tournament. The top four players including ties in The Open are invited to the next year's Masters. Matsuyama tied for sixth place, missing a tie for third place by one stroke.

Sergio Garcia moved to three over with a 68.

Richard Sterne gained 51 places with his own 68.

Johnson Wagner holed out for a 73.

the fourth with one leg bent double outside the trap, no doubt thanks to his extensive warming-up exercises on the range.

More often, however, he could not save himself. Out in 39, he did collect his second birdie of the day at the 13th, but a poor second shot cost a bogey at the 14th, he left a shot in a bunker at the 16th for a double-bogey and missed a short putt for par at the 17th. He had fallen from three under to three over, but while his challenge may have faltered, he retains the affection of the public. Applauded out of his favourite restaurant in North Berwick on Friday night, he was applauded into it on Saturday evening.

There were other tales of trauma, Darren Clarke not collecting a birdie in his 76 and Martin Laird, Scotland's main hope going into the weekend, collapsing to an 81. He first tangled with the Muirfield rough for a 9, including two penalty shots for unplayables, at the third hole, and then at the 10th was docked a shot for not informing his playing partner or the referee when he touched his ball to identify it. He had a double-bogey there and

Martin Laird had a difficult day, including a 9 on the third hole.

another at the 17th, so three holes had cost him 22 strokes.

Japan's talented 21-year-old Hideki Matsuyama also received a penalty stroke, for slow play, when he recorded a second bad time at the 17th hole. The former double winner of the Asia Pacific Amateur Championship turned professional in April and won two of his first five starts on the Japan PGA Tour and was making an impressive debut in The Open when he hit into the crowd. He was allowed time to move spectators and to walk forward on his line to view his shot, but the timing official still reckoned he took two minutes and 12 seconds once it was his turn to play. Matsuyama's playing partner, Johnson Wagner, pleaded his case in the recorder's hut with chief referee David Rickman, but to no avail. A 71 became

Martin Kaymer was on five over par.

Francesco Molinari had a 72 to be two over.

Keegan Bradley returned a 70 to be six over.

Ernie Els scored a 70 to be five over.

a 72 and Matsuyama dropped back to three over par.

A cooler, overcast morning meant the course retained more moisture for longer after the greens had been hand-watered overnight and Richard Sterne and Sergio Garcia took advantage by zipping up the standings with three-under-par 68s. It was a score matched later in the day by Mahan, who jumped from a tie for 20th into a tie for second place. For the second Major Championship in a row he would play in the final pairing on Sunday after accompanying Mickelson at Merion, where he finished tied for fourth.

Mahan started his round with two contrasting birdies, the first thanks to an approach with a wedge that finished a foot from the hole, while at the second he holed a left-to-right putt from over 50 feet away. He dropped a shot at the fourth, as he would at the 13th, but also birdied the ninth, where he reached the green with two running 3-irons, the 15th, where he holed from 12 feet, and the 17th, where he holed from 20 feet from short of the green.

In Britain, Mahan is remembered for dunking a chip and losing to Graeme McDowell at the conclusion of the 2010 Ryder Cup at Celtic Manor. To the American it is ancient history, as he showed by

Round of the Day: Hunter Mahan - 68

OFFICIAL SCORECARD
THE OPEN CHAMPIONSHIP 2013
MUIRFIELD

Hunter MAHAN
Game 32
Saturday 20 July at 1:35pm

FOR R&A USE ONLY	212		ROUND 3	
36 HOLE TOTAL	144		54 HOLE TOTAL	
THIS ROUND	68			212
54 HOLE TOTAL	212			

ROUND 3

Hole	1	2	3	4	5	6	7	8	9	Out
Yards	447	364	377	226	559	461	184	441	554	3613
Par	4	4	4	3	5	4	3	4	5	36
Score	3	3	4	4	5	4	3	4	4	34

10	11	12	13	14	15	16	17	18	In	Total
469	387	379	190	475	448	186	575	470	3579	7192
4	4	4	3	4	4	3	5	4	35	71
4	4	4	4	4	3	3	4	4	34	68

Signature of Marker

Signature of Competitor
Hunter Mahan

Noteworthy

- **Hole 1:** 3-iron, wedge, one putt from one foot
- **Hole 2:** 5-iron, wedge, one putt from 50 feet
- **Hole 4:** 3-iron, sand wedge from bunker, two putts
- **Hole 9:** 3-iron, 3-iron, two putts from 20 feet
- **Hole 15:** 4-iron, wedge, one putt from 12 feet
- **Hole 17:** Driver, 8-iron, 5-iron, one putt from left of the green from 20 feet

Mahan plays his approach to the 18th hole.

In the Words of the Competitors…

"

"I didn't strike it great yesterday, so I wanted to have a little practice session before I played today. And it went well, I thought. I hit it pretty good today."

—Phil Mickelson

"I'm a competitor. You're not going to lie down until the 72nd hole. That's just the nature of what's going on out there."

—Ernie Els

"Being in the first or second, last groups there, to have everybody following you and seeing all the scores and everything, it can be overwhelming. But there's no rules in this game, you can kind of do whatever you want."

—Hunter Mahan

"I just want to play a round I'm happy with."

—Jordan Spieth

"I hit a lot more fairways today. I hit it in the right side of the holes. And I gave myself a lot of easy pars, which I hadn't been doing all week."

—Keegan Bradley

"I finally felt like I knew what I was doing out there."

—Sergio Garcia

"

Round Three Hole Summary

HOLE	PAR	YARDS	EAGLES	BIRDIES	PARS	BOGEYS	D.BOGEYS	OTHER	RANK	AVERAGE
1	4	447	0	5	67	11	1	0	12	4.095
2	4	364	0	11	63	10	0	0	15	3.988
3	4	377	0	6	55	19	3	1	7	4.286
4	3	226	0	2	39	31	11	1	1	3.643
5	5	559	2	24	41	17	0	0	17	4.869
6	4	461	1	6	42	28	6	1	3	4.417
7	3	184	0	12	61	10	0	1	14	3.012
8	4	441	0	4	51	26	3	0	4	4.333
9	5	554	4	47	25	8	0	0	18	4.440
OUT	**36**	**3,613**	**7**	**117**	**444**	**160**	**24**	**4**		**37.083**
10	4	469	0	5	51	26	2	0	6	4.298
11	4	387	0	11	56	16	1	0	13	4.083
12	4	379	0	14	62	7	1	0	16	3.940
13	3	190	0	11	49	20	4	0	8	3.202
14	4	475	0	10	53	18	3	0	10	4.167
15	4	448	0	7	56	20	1	0	9	4.179
16	3	186	0	1	49	27	7	0	2	3.476
17	5	575	0	10	54	18	2	0	11	5.143
18	4	470	0	5	51	26	1	1	5	4.321
IN	**35**	**3,579**	**0**	**74**	**481**	**178**	**22**	**1**		**36.810**
TOTAL	**71**	**7,192**	**7**	**191**	**925**	**338**	**46**	**5**		**73.893**

Ian Poulter wondered if five over was too far back.

getting up and down from a bunker at the last. "I don't need any redemption or anything like that," he said. "I don't play golf for revenge or to make up for anything. I play because I really like to play and the ultimate challenge is Major Championship golf."

He had a simple answer to why he has not yet won a Major. "Not being good enough," he said. "Probably my short game hasn't been as strong as it needed to be, but I'm chipping and putting great and comfortable with my game. I'm excited about the opportunity."

Three men who still felt they had a good opportunity were Poulter, Mickelson and Stenson. The Swede was playing with Jimenez in the final pairing of the day and after two 70s he was hoping for something better than a 74. Unusually, Stenson did not take advantage of the par 5s and made only one birdie, at the second, but had parred 11

Angel Cabrera was in touch on one over par.

holes in a row before three-putting at the last to fall four behind. "Overall, I was happy with the way I was hanging in there, but I needed to pick up one or two on the back nine," said the Swede.

Poulter was eight strokes back after a 75. "Leaves me a little work to do tomorrow," he admitted. "But my game is in shape, and if I roll in a few putts tomorrow, I can run back up the board."

Mickelson had a lengthy session with his coach, Butch Harmon, on the practice range on Saturday morning. He then went out and scored a 72. "Anything around par today was a good round," he said. "I think I'll have to play a good round tomorrow, but I think it's right there." Three bogeys in his last six holes, combined with Westwood getting to three under, meant he ended up five behind, so overnight he may have amended his forecast that: "If I can shoot something in the 60s, I think that will be enough."

At two over par, Phil Mickelson was well within reach.

Excerpts
FROM Press
THE

"On the 16th green at Muirfield, a flock of sea gulls were fighting over a big crust of bread, swooping, shrieking, and depriving one another of the loot as golf fans, pressed tight against the ropes, pointed and chuckled. The timing seemed just right considering that the two men in the process of hitting tee shots, Lee Westwood and Tiger Woods, were also scrapping over The Open lead."

—Karen Crouse, *The New York Times*

"Mickelson is hoping that, having waited an eternity for a win on British soil, another victory will roll up right behind it. It took him two decades to card his first UK win, at the Scottish Open last week. But as this most testing of Opens reaches its conclusion, he has ensured he remains in a position to pounce."

—Moira Gordon, *Scotland on Sunday*

"Before the start of the tournament, there was no shortage of praise from the world's best players for the narrow, rock-like fairways and slippery greens, both gently whipped by eddying zephyrs, as a test of their skill and intuition, yet that kind view did not altogether survive the cut. By the weekend, the judgment had hardened, like the ground (and, having knelt on it from inside the ropes in front of the gallery, this observer would rate it as unyielding as a kneeling board in a confessional)."

—Kevin Mitchell, *The Observer*

A 70 for Todd Hamilton.

Shingo Katayama posted a 69.

But a year ago Ernie Els had come back from six behind to win the Claret Jug when Scott, the 54-hole leader at Lytham, had let a four-stroke lead with four holes to play evaporate with four bogeys. Increasingly confident in his preparations for Major Championships, however, Scott won an epic duel with Cabrera to win the Masters at the second extra hole in April. And after nine practice rounds at Muirfield, he had quietly worked his way into fourth place after a third round of 70 with three birdies and two bogeys.

Scott said: "I said the other day it would be a fairy tale if it were to happen. They do occasionally happen, so I'm not counting myself out. It is a good feeling to sit here in this position, completely different to last year. I go out tomorrow not carrying the weight of the lead or not having won a Major."

Woods made only two birdies, one at the second which briefly tied him for the lead with Jimenez, and the other at the ninth. Westwood dropped a shot at the third and did well to get up and down at the par-3 fourth. Although being shortened to 198 yards with use of a forward tee to the right of the back markers to improve the line to the front-left pin position, the fourth ranked the hardest hole on the course in the third round. There were only two birdies and Woods made one of the 43 scores over par when he failed to get up and down from a bunker.

Paul Lawrie had a 70 after a brief trip home on Friday evening.

Carl Pettersson had a 70 for seven over.

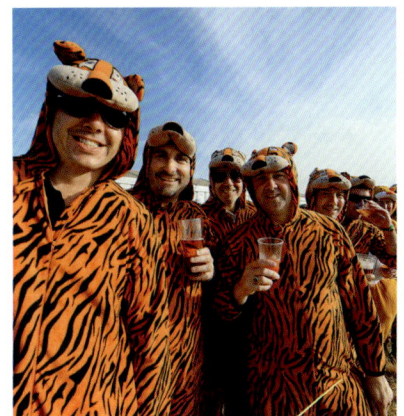

Westwood went on to eagle the fifth, having hit a driver off the deck for his second shot for the second day running, and then played an exquisite bunker rescue at the sixth. A 9-iron to five feet at the seventh put him three in front of Woods, but he then three-putted the eighth and had a 6 at the ninth to the 4 of Woods, so they were tied again. But Woods was to come home in one over, while Westwood looked increasingly comfortable with his game, not least in hitting a 6-iron to four feet at the 14th.

Walking every step of the way was his son, Sam. "He's only been to one tournament before where he's walked round and that was in Sweden last year when I won by five or six," Westwood said. "He'll be wanting commission." Having sold his home in Worksop over the winter and set up a new base in America, perhaps it would be ironic if he returned home to a British heatwave and won the title he wanted most. "Little did I know when I moved to Florida that I was acclimatising for The Open in Scotland," he joked.

The 40-year-old admitted that night he would visualise holding the Claret Jug but would be ready to focus on his game come his Sunday tee-time. This was his 62nd Major Championship. No one in the field had played more without winning one. The only other time he had led after 54 holes was at the Masters in 2010 when he was unable to hold off a charging left-handed American by the name of Mickelson.

LOOKING FOR THE MURRAY MAGIC

By Art Spander

British success was everywhere in a glorious summer. Down Under, The Lions in Rugby Union; in the United States, Justin Rose claiming their golf Open; at Wimbledon, at last, Andy Murray, the Scot in the long-awaited breakthrough; in the Test matches, for The Ashes; in the hills of France, Chris Froome pedalling towards victory in Le Tour.

How fitting, how perfectly scripted, heading into the final day of the 142nd Open Championship, an Englishman would be in the lead. And not just any Englishman, arguably the most accomplished Englishman of the recent generation.

Lee Westwood, who had done everything in a career from helping acquire Ryder Cup victories to achieving the world number one ranking to moving to the United States — after insisting he would remain on the European Tour — to offering a sense of humour about as subtle as some of the breaks in the Muirfield greens.

Pressure holding the 54-hole lead when he never had won a Major? "Actually," he said that Saturday evening, "I'm not in a high-pressure situation because I'm going to have dinner, and I'm so good with a knife and fork now that I don't feel any pressure at all. I might go the Andy Murray route and have 50 pieces of sushi or something like that.

"I'll think about winning The Open Championship at some stage I'm sure. I don't see anything wrong with that, to picture yourself holding the Claret Jug and seeing your name at the top of the leaderboard."

It certainly was there on Saturday as Westwood, so often the nearly man in the Majors, with seconds at The Open and Masters, out-duelled his playing partner, one Tiger Woods, to move ahead. There he was marching along the dusty fairways towards a one-under-par 70 and a two-shot lead over Woods and Hunter Mahan.

"Even though I haven't won a Major," advised Westwood, "I know what it takes to win one." Absolutely. It takes sublime play and a break now and then. It takes English coolness best described by the French term *sang froid*. At 40, Westwood was experienced enough. A perfect age at the perfect place.

Golf can be the most frustrating of games, a sport in which you have no control over an opponent and sometimes none over yourself; a sport in which a three-foot putt counts the same number of strokes as a 300-yard drive; a sport which, as Forgan wrote, is a trial of honour and a test of character. "It's just a case of going out Sunday," reminded Westwood, "and having the confidence in my game, which I've got."

What he didn't have was the ability to master Muirfield or his own failings. For the longest time, Westwood was recognised as an excellent long game player but lacking in the short game, especially with the putter.

But in Florida, where Westwood had relocated with his family as he chased the dream he tried to make everyone believe he wasn't chasing — "I'm a philosophical person," Lee said — his putting had improved. Westwood had been helped by one of his neighbours, Ian Baker-Finch,

the Australian who won the 1991 Open at Royal Birkdale.

"There's a little more connection between my arms and body," said Westwood of his newly developed skill on the greens. "Ian has given me a couple of tips on getting tension out of my arms."

Westwood's new instructor, Sean Foley, was also the man who had been assisting Woods and Mahan, so had the three men at the top after three rounds. Among Foley's other pupils was Rose, who, although missing the cut at Muirfield, a month earlier had become the first Englishman in 43 years to win the American Open.

Beginning the third round a shot behind Spain's Miguel Angel Jimenez, Westwood, with his white trousers and orange shirt, eyes covered by sunglasses, went one over with a bogey on the third.

His 45-foot eagle putt on the par-5 fifth moved him to one under for the round, where he stayed with three birdies and three bogeys, one of those with a 20-foot putt at 16.

"I love playing The Open Championship," said Westwood, feeling appropriately elated. "This is the biggest tournament of the year for me, being a Brit, and it being played in Britain, so why not enjoy it?"

He tried hard. But as John Hopkins wrote in *The Times*, as Westwood putted well enough but required too many shots with his irons and woods, "His strengths were weaknesses, his weaknesses were strengths." Soon, his lead was nonexistent.

Eventually Phil Mickelson, who wasn't supposed to have the game for The Open, would climb into first and Westwood on Sunday would shoot his worst round of the week, a 75, and fall to a tie for third.

"I didn't play well enough," was Westwood's succinct analysis. "I didn't play badly, but I didn't play great. It's a tough course, and you've got to have your 'A' game. I finished in the top three of a Major Championship."

For the eighth time. With no wins.

"For me," Westwood pointed out, "to be last off in The Open was a new experience. It had never happened to me before on a Sunday. I keep putting myself in contention. I never second-guess myself. You just do what feels right at the time."

Mark O'Meara, the 1998 Open winner who in 2013 at age 56 made the cut, believed Westwood will be a factor in future Opens.

"He has a lot of good years ahead," said O'Meara. "You can be a good player into your 40s, especially as good a ball-striker as Lee Westwood is."

And was through three rounds at Muirfield.

THE OPEN CHAMPIONSHIP

Fourth Round

Phil Brings Home the Claret Jug

By Andy Farrell

With a score of 66 at Muirfield, Phil Mickelson finally wins The Open with a dramatic late charge.

Has an Open Championship ever been won with such a dramatic, daring late charge as that produced by Phil Mickelson at Muirfield in 2013? It was typical of the man. So often he has gone for broke. Sometimes it has come off spectacularly. More times he has been the one to crack, ending up in pieces on the locker room floor. At the seaside links of Britain it was always the case. Until now. Until a burst of genius that resulted in four birdies in the last six holes and the American holding the Claret Jug.

With six holes to play, Mickelson was not out of it by any means, but the attention focused elsewhere — Adam Scott was surging; Lee Westwood was still trying to cling to the lead he held from overnight; Henrik Stenson was lurking; Ian Poulter had sparkled but burnt himself out. Poulter's

Mickelson celebrated holing his birdie putt at the 18th.

clubhouse lead was at one over, the score Mickelson held after 12 holes. It was time to go out and win the 142nd Open Championship.

Mickelson felt something, anything under par would win and while all round were concerned with bogeys, avoiding them or settling for them, the left-hander was talking birdies. Two at the 13th and 14th holes were the foundations of his charge. A delayed effect meant by the time he walked onto the 17th green he was now in the lead on his own. A two-putt there, after two mighty blows to reach the par 5 that he considered his best shots of the week, followed by a glorious closing 3 at the 18th gave him a three-stroke victory.

Suddenly, the American was clear at the top of the leaderboard. Four pairs of players still had to complete their rounds, but they were now playing for second place. Stenson claimed it on level par, leaving the Champion Golfer of the Year, as Mickelson predicted, as the only player to finish in red figures, with Poulter, Scott and Westwood sharing third place at one over.

"I've always tried to go out and get it," Mickelson said. "I don't want anybody to hand it to me.

"Muirfield does discriminate — it only allows in the greats. And there is absolutely no doubt of Phil Mickelson's credentials after yesterday."

—James Corrigan,
The Daily Telegraph

"One of the greatest final rounds in a Major. Two of the best shots he ever struck with a 3-wood. The third leg of the Grand Slam. Phil Mickelson never imagined any of this happening at The Open. No wonder he never took his hand off the base of that silver Claret Jug as he talked about the best Sunday he ever had at a Major. Five shots out of the lead, Mickelson blew past Tiger Woods, caught up with Lee Westwood and Masters Champion Adam Scott, and won golf's oldest championship with the lowest final round in his 80 Majors."

—Doug Ferguson,
The Associated Press

"Matt Fitzpatrick, the 18-year-old who looks like a 13-year-old in his gym kit, had the glory of a round with Fred Couples. Like a kid playing with his dad. Or possibly, with all due respect to Fred, his granddad. Couples, shorter than you might expect, still a handsome devil, still with an aura, walked like a Highland laird and was kindly to the boy, bumping his arm, high-fiving him as they sank their par putts and left the course."

—Melanie Reid, *The Times*

Adam Scott, bunkered at the 16th, again led The Open before four bogeys in a row.

I want to go and get it and I did that today. Just to capture this Championship and be a part of history of The Open, the event that has been the hardest in my career to capture, it doesn't matter how, but certainly to birdie four of the last six is awesome."

Once again Muirfield had produced not just a thrilling Championship but a winner of the highest quality. With, finally, an Open crown to go with his three Masters triumphs and a US PGA Championship, Mickelson ensured the 16 Opens played here have only seen one winner who is not a multiple Major Champion.

Yet none of those impressive names who feature on the roll of honour at this treacherous East Lothian links had ever scored as low as 66 in the final round. Gary Player's 68, including a double-bogey at the last, was previously the best, but Mickelson finished in style

Mickelson tees-off at the fourth after a slow but steady start.

Fourth Round Leaders

HOLE	1	2	3	4	5	6	7	8	9	10	11	12	13	14	15	16	17	18	TOTAL
PAR	4	4	4	3	5	4	3	4	5	4	4	4	3	4	4	3	5	4	
Phil Mickelson	4	4	4	3	(4)	4	3	4	(4)	[5]	4	4	(2)	(3)	4	3	(4)	(3)	66-281
Henrik Stenson	(3)	4	(3)	3	5	4	3	[5]	(4)	4	4	[5]	[4]	4	4	3	(4)	4	70-284
Ian Poulter	4	4	[5]	3	(4)	4	3	4	**(3)**	(3)	(3)	(3)	3	4	4	[4]	5	4	67-285
Adam Scott	[5]	4	4	[4]	5	4	(2)	(3)	(4)	4	(3)	4	[4]	[5]	[5]	[4]	5	(3)	72-285
Lee Westwood	4	4	[5]	3	(4)	4	[4]	[5]	5	5	4	4	[4]	4	4	[4]	5	4	75-285

Lee Westwood struggled on Sunday after starting in the lead.

when he hit a 6-iron off the shoulder of the bunker to the left of the green to 12 feet and then curled in the putt.

There, right at the denouement, was a clue as to how Mickelson had curbed his naturally aggressive style just enough. Not to fight the terrain and the elements but use them to his benefit, the eternal secret to links golf. After a thunderous ovation for the man who had already endeared himself to the local gallery by winning the Scottish Open the previous Sunday at Castle Stuart, Mickelson left the 18th green with his arm round the shoulders of his trusted bagman, Jim "Bones" Mackay. For the British-born caddie, who has stood alongside Mickelson for his entire career, tears of joy flowed freely. There were embraces for Butch Harmon, his coach, and Steve Loy, his manager, and then the family, wife Amy, daughters Amanda and Sophia and son Evan.

"This is just an amazing feeling winning this great Championship," Mickelson said. "To play probably the best round of my career, playing some of the best shots I've ever hit, certainly putting better than I've ever putted. I knew I needed my 'A' game today, I needed to show up and play some of the best golf of my life. And I did. It's a day I'll always cherish."

His victory was only the second for a left-hander in the Championship and came 50 years on from Sir Bob Charles' win at Royal Lytham and St Annes. This was his 20th appearance in The Open, equalling Darren Clarke's record for the longest wait to claim the Claret Jug. Clarke was born and bred on links golf, but it has always been an alien concept to the man who grew up in Southern California.

Something clicked when his first-nine charge at Royal St George's in 2011 gave Clarke a fright before the Northern Irishman finally won the title he craved most. By winning the title he thought he might never win, Mickelson became fifth oldest ever winner at 43 and, following Clarke and Ernie

Zach Johnson, two over, thought this putt would fall. When it didn't, he did.

Els, a third successive winner in his 40s. In fact, the last three Opens have seen three of the oldest seven Champions.

Age hardly mattered as Mickelson swept to victory. If his timing had been a little off at Royal St George's, this time it was perfect. Only two other players managed to play the last six holes in as low as two under and neither Justin Leonard nor Stephen Gallacher was playing with the leaders. Scott, who made four birdies in five holes to take the lead on his own at two under after 11 holes, suffered a nightmare streak that was reminiscent of a year earlier at Lytham when he had four bogeys in a row from the 13th. A birdie at the last meant he played the last six in three over, as did Ryan Moore.

Westwood, who briefly regained a share of the lead standing on the

Henrik Stenson at the 15th hole on the way to a 70 and the runner-up spot.

13th tee, played the last six in two over, as did Zach Johnson and Angel Cabrera. Hunter Mahan, who was playing in the last pairing on Sunday for the second Major running, finished with one over on the last six, as Poulter had done earlier. Tiger Woods, who never seriously threatened on the final day, and Stenson both played the last six in level par.

"The wow factor just kind of happened," Mickelson added. "It wasn't like I was trying to force birdies, I was just trying to hit good shots. And I made a bunch of putts. It's as good as I've ever putted in my career. I putted these greens phenomenal and the birdies just kind of happened.

"Links greens, I think, have been the reason I have not been in contention very often over here. More so than the ball-striking, although the penalty for missed shots in The Open Championship is so severe and it took me awhile to figure that out. I've started to

Fourth Round Scores	
Players Under Par	15
Players At Par	7
Players Over Par	62

Low Scores

Low First Nine	
Stewart Cink	32
Low Second Nine	
Phil Mickelson	32
Bo Van Pelt	32
Low Round	
Phil Mickelson	66

Tiger Woods never threatened after bogeys at the first and, here, at the fourth.

Round Four Hole Summary

HOLE	PAR	YARDS	EAGLES	BIRDIES	PARS	BOGEYS	D.BOGEYS	OTHER	RANK	AVERAGE
1	4	447	0	8	59	15	2	0	10	4.131
2	4	364	1	10	64	7	2	0	14	3.988
3	4	377	0	12	58	13	1	0	11	4.036
4	3	226	0	0	54	27	2	1	1	3.405
5	5	559	1	28	44	10	1	0	17	4.786
6	4	461	0	4	49	27	4	0	3	4.369
7	3	184	0	14	60	9	1	0	16	2.964
8	4	441	0	5	50	25	4	0	4	4.333
9	5	554	5	35	31	11	2	0	18	4.643
OUT	**36**	**3,613**	**7**	**116**	**469**	**144**	**19**	**1**		**36.655**
10	4	469	0	3	51	26	3	1	2	4.381
11	4	387	0	13	57	13	1	0	13	4.024
12	4	379	0	17	52	13	0	2	11	4.036
13	3	190	0	9	52	20	2	1	7	3.214
14	4	475	0	6	52	21	5	0	5	4.298
15	4	448	0	7	61	13	3	0	9	4.143
16	3	186	0	4	55	23	2	0	6	3.274
17	5	575	1	17	50	14	2	0	14	4.988
18	4	470	0	8	55	17	4	0	8	4.202
IN	**35**	**3,579**	**1**	**84**	**485**	**160**	**22**	**4**		**36.560**
TOTAL	**71**	**7,192**	**8**	**200**	**954**	**304**	**41**	**5**		**73.214**

1997 Champion Justin Leonard came home in 33 and tied 13th.

play shots more effectively, but it is so different from what I grew up playing. I was wondering if I would ever develop the skills to win this Championship. That's what makes this so special."

No one had ever done the double of winning the Scottish Open and The Open in successive weeks. Mickelson had won the BellSouth Classic prior to the 2006 Masters. He said victory at Castle Stuart had given him the confidence to believe he could play his best golf in links conditions.

Although there were as many scores in the 60s in the final round as there were in rounds two and three put together (nine), Mickelson's 66 will stand the test of time as one of the greatest in Open history. It was the lowest score in the last round by a Champion since Leonard's 65 at Royal Troon in 1997 and matched the lowest score of the week, by Zach Johnson all the way back on Thursday morning. In the overcast conditions and after more

Matthew Fitzpatrick with Fred Couples at the 18th.

hand-watering overnight, the course yielded some low scores early on. But with the wind again from the east and gusting up to 20mph at times in the afternoon, Mickelson's effort stood in stark contrast to what the other leaders produced: Westwood and Mahan 75s, Woods a 74, Scott and Johnson 72s. Poulter with his 67 and Stenson and Hideki Maruyama with 70s were the only other players under par who finished in the top 10.

Harmon, who was also coaching Woods, Stewart Cink and Greg Norman when they won The Open, thought Mickelson's performance outstripped Norman's 64 at Sandwich in 1993 to beat Sir Nick Faldo and Bernhard Langer. "I always thought when Greg won it was the best round to win an Open," Harmon said. "But I think this tops it. When you consider the course was playing so tough, so hard and fast, and the circumstances, to go out and suck it up in the way he did was phenomenal."

It was another quality leaderboard here, with

Hunter Mahan, 75, had started with high hopes.

④

Excerpts FROM THE Press

Eduardo De La Riva (left) and Jonas Blixt both finished their maiden Opens with 69s.

"After completing a dream double on Scottish soil by following up his victory at Castle Stuart last week by claiming the title at the 142nd Open Championship at Muirfield, the big American's popularity has just gone through the roof in the home of golf."

—Martin Dempster, *The Scotsman*

"For a spell, it was just like being back in the bear pit of the Ryder Cup at Medinah as Poulter, runner-up in the 2008 Open, tapped into those aggressive, adrenaline-charged reserves. The gallus swagger was in full flow as he marched purposefully down the fairway with his chest puffed out about 40 yards in front of him."

—Nick Rodger, *The Herald*

"This latest moment of Major glory must go down as his greatest yet. For Phil can now claim to be the complete golfer who has finally mastered the links style."

—Euan McLean, *Daily Record*

"Breakfast at the Mickelsons isn't like ours. What we say during Sunday breakfast: 'Pass the flapjacks, will ya.' What Phil Mickelson says during Sunday breakfast: 'I'm gonna go out and get a Claret Jug today.'"

—Gene Wojciechowski, ESPN.com

"Adam Scott admitted he 'wasted' another chance of Open success, a year after his infamous collapse."

—Simon Bird, *Daily Mirror*

Woods, the world number one, finishing in a tie for sixth place, alongside Johnson and Matsuyama, the young Japanese rookie who collected his second Major top-10 finish in a row despite the one-stroke penalty for slow play the previous day. Brandt Snedeker, the only player other than Mickelson to have two rounds in the 60s, was tied for 11th, while Gallacher was the leading Scot, tied for 21st place. Matthew Fitzpatrick, the reigning Boys Amateur Champion won the Silver Medal as the leading amateur after finishing on 10 over par, one behind his last-round playing partner, Fred Couples, but five strokes in front of Jimmy Mullen, the 19-year-old from Royal North Devon, who was the only other amateur to make the cut.

It was no surprise when Amy Mickelson reported her ultra-positive husband had left their room at the Marine Hotel in North Berwick that morning with the words: "I'm going to go and bring home the Claret Jug." Five behind starting the day, the world number five started with four pars, although an incident on the first fairway showed how relaxed he was. For two weeks, at Castle Stuart and during The Open, his caddie Mackay had told him: "Slow down. Let's enjoy this." When Bones rushed off down the fairway, Mickelson hauled him back and reminded him of their mantra.

Championship Hole Summary

HOLE	PAR	YARDS	EAGLES	BIRDIES	PARS	BOGEYS	D.BOGEYS	OTHER	RANK	AVERAGE
1	4	447	0	30	304	115	22	6	9	4.312
2	4	364	1	76	322	73	4	1	15	4.013
3	4	377	0	73	311	83	9	1	13	4.069
4	3	226	0	26	272	147	27	5	2	3.398
5	5	559	10	168	221	70	8	0	17	4.786
6	4	461	1	25	268	153	25	4	3	4.397
7	3	184	0	57	328	76	13	2	11	3.109
8	4	441	0	28	260	158	26	4	1	4.408
9	5	554	15	201	182	63	11	3	18	4.714
OUT	**36**	**3,613**	**27**	**684**	**2,468**	**938**	**145**	**26**		**37.198**
10	4	469	0	33	266	146	26	4	6	4.373
11	4	387	0	64	326	72	11	2	12	4.078
12	4	379	0	75	312	73	12	3	14	4.067
13	3	190	0	50	270	129	22	4	10	3.286
14	4	475	0	31	259	161	21	3	5	4.383
15	4	448	1	38	253	154	26	3	6	4.373
16	3	186	0	23	287	142	18	5	8	3.360
17	5	575	10	103	266	82	14	0	16	4.973
18	4	470	0	33	265	144	27	6	4	4.387
IN	**35**	**3,579**	**11**	**450**	**2,504**	**1,103**	**177**	**30**		**37.280**
TOTAL	**71**	**7,192**	**38**	**1,134**	**4,972**	**2,041**	**322**	**56**		**74.478**

In the rough for two at the par-5 fifth, Mickelson played a delightful recovery with a sand wedge from 80 yards to four feet and made the first of his six birdies. Otherwise he continued to two-putt his way around the first nine, though having found the green with a 6-iron at the ninth he had another birdie and was out in 34. "It was a cool feeling when I made birdie there to get back to level for the tournament," he said. "I knew I was in contention." His only bogey of the day promptly followed when he put a 5-iron into the front-left bunker at the 10th and took a 5. At one over par, he was still four off the lead.

While both Woods and Scott, playing in the penultimate pairing, bogeyed the first, Stenson made the best start with birdies at the first, holing from over 45 feet, and the third, where his putt was considerably shorter. Westwood parred the first two but then pulled his tee shot at the third

Stephen Gallacher was the leading Scot, tied for 21st place.

Matt Kuchar, 71, improved by a stroke each day.

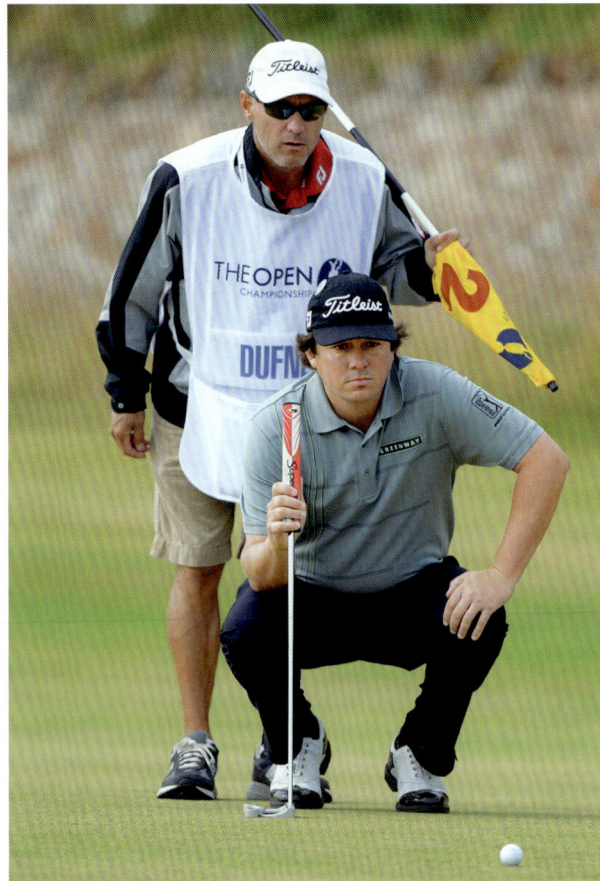
Jason Dufner finished strongly with a 67.

into rough and ended up with a bogey. Despite driving into a bunker at the fifth, he claimed a birdie-4 to get back to three under, but his troubles started at the short seventh. Between clubs at a hole playing its full yardage of 198 yards but downwind, he elected to hit a 9-iron and came up short in the front bunker. Worse, he was plugged under the lip and could not escape first time. More bunker trouble led to another bogey at the eighth and only a par at the ninth. He was still at one under, but it felt like three dropped shots in a row. "That halted my momentum a bit," he said.

Poulter, who had birdied the fifth, started a Ryder Cup-style run by holing from 12 feet for an eagle at the ninth, then made putts for birdie of 30 feet, over the little hump that protects the front of the

green at the 10th, 18 feet on the 11th and 16 feet on the 12th. "The excitement, the atmosphere, the fans were giving me a lot of electricity out there and pumping me up," he said. "It's nice to be in that position when you are in front of a home crowd and running up the leaderboard.

Having started the day eight strokes behind, Poulter had got himself up into a tie for second at level par but there the run ended. "I hit a fantastic shot into 13 to about 12 feet and missed the putt," he said. "I'm a leaderboard watcher and obviously I realised if I could post a number, sometimes it's a good position to be in." At Birkdale in 2008, he holed a superb putt on the final green but then had to watch Padraig Harrington sweep past him.

An excited Ian Poulter picked up six shots in eight holes.

Ian Poulter
Another Exciting Charge

He was eight shots back with 18 holes remaining. "Realistically," agreed Ian Poulter, "do you really think you've got a chance to run straight through and nick it?"

Poulter, the Englishman known for his emotional play in the Ryder Cup, said he thought of Paul Lawrie coming from 10 behind in the 1999 Open at Carnoustie. Then he made birdies. Loads of them. And an eagle.

The golfer who criticised the greens after the first round, implying several were reminiscent of miniature golf on a carpet, picked up six shots in eight holes, with a birdie on the fifth, an eagle-3 on the ninth and birdies on 10, 11 and 12. When he starts making putts, few players create more excitement, perhaps only the eventual Champion, Phil Mickelson.

Poulter would bogey the par-3 16th but still finish with a four-under 67 and finish in a three-way tie for third at 285 with Lee Westwood and Adam Scott.

"A couple of putts slipped by out there," said the 33-year-old. "They may have been what was required for me to get my hands on the trophy."

An inveterate user of Twitter, Poulter sent out, "Great playing Mickelson. I gave it a good go. That's all you can do on a Sunday @ The Open. Thanks for the support."

Later he said correctly, "I was right in the mix. This tournament always creates a lot of drama."

It did in 2013 because of rounds like Ian Poulter's final effort.

—Art Spander

Hideki Matsuyama closed with a 70 to tie for sixth place.

Now he bogeyed the 16th and a 67 left him at one over par.

Westwood was attempting not just to win his first Major Championship but, after Justin Rose's US Open victory, give England a transatlantic double for the first time since 1909 (JH Taylor and George Sargent). At one under after nine, he was still tied for the lead with Stenson and Scott. The Swede did damage to his cause when he went over the green at the 12th for the first of two bogeys in a row.

Scott, however, was tantalisingly within reach of a second Major of the year and that fairy-tale redemption after losing so cruelly at Lytham. With Woods unable to get the pace of the greens, Scott birdied the seventh, the eighth and the ninth and then added a fourth in five holes at the 11th from four feet. At two under, he now led by one from Westwood.

But then four shots disappeared as he missed the green at the 13th, putted over the 14th green, three-putted the 15th and found a bunker at the 16th. "I let a great chance slip," Scott said. "I was right there, so it was disappointing, but I lived up to my expectation of putting myself in contention."

Woods flickered to life by holing a long putt at the 12th and then hitting a wonderful approach at the 14th to six inches. But any momentum he had built up was lost when he three-putted the next green. "I had a hard time adjusting to the speed of the greens," he said. "I left myself a couple of long lag putts early on when it was really blowing and left them way short."

Westwood's downfall came at the two short holes on the second nine as he tangled with the rough short and right of the 13th green and also bogeyed the 16th. "I hit some poor tee shots, including at the third, the seventh, 13 and 16," he said. "I didn't hit good shots when it mattered."

For the eighth time he had finished in the top three at a Major, but for the second time when leading after 54 holes he was beaten by Mickelson.

Round of the Day: **Phil Mickelson – 66**

OFFICIAL SCORECARD
THE OPEN CHAMPIONSHIP 2013
MUIRFIELD

Phil MICKELSON ✓
Game 38
Sunday 21 July at 1:30pm

	FOR R&A USE ONLY 362	ROUND 4
54 HOLE TOTAL	215	72 HOLE TOTAL
THIS ROUND	66	
72 HOLE TOTAL	281	281

VERIFIED

ROUND 4

Hole	1	2	3	4	5	6	7	8	9	Out	10	11	12	13	14	15	16	17	18	In	Total
Yards	447	364	377	226	559	461	184	441	554	3613	469	387	379	190	475	448	186	575	470	3579	7192
Par	4	4	4	3	5	4	3	4	5	36	4	4	4	3	4	4	3	5	4	35	71
Score	4	4	4	3	4	4	3	4	4	34	5	4	4	2	3	4	3	4	3	32	66

Signature
of Marker

Signature of
Competitor
Phil Mickelson

Noteworthy

- **Hole 5:** 3-wood, 9-iron, two putts from 50 feet
- **Hole 9:** 4-iron, 6-iron, two putts from 30 feet
- **Hole 10:** 4-iron, 5-iron, sand wedge from greenside bunker, two putts from 30 feet
- **Hole 13:** 5-iron, one putt from 10 feet
- **Hole 14:** 4-iron, 9-iron, one putt from 20 feet
- **Hole 17:** 3-wood, 3-wood, two putts from 40 feet
- **Hole 18:** hybrid, 6-iron, one putt from 12 feet

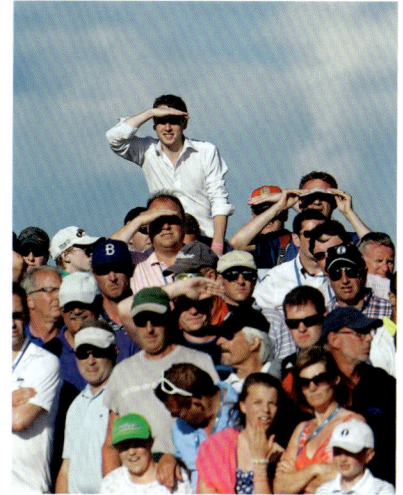

Championship Totals	
Rounds Under Par	58
Rounds At Par	33
Rounds Over Par	384

Mickelson tees-off at the 15th hole after making a move by birdieing the previous two.

Henrik Stenson
'We all know what we're longing for'

Henrik Stenson began the final round hoping to become the first male Swede to win a Major golf championship. Two birdies in the first three holes did nothing to alter the thought.

Even after making back-to-back bogeys on 12 and 13 to fall back to even for the round, the 37-year-old Stenson was not discouraged.

"The key to success," he said, "is to keep moving forward. I didn't let the bogeys set me back, and I finished off in good style."

Which meant four pars and a birdie, a 4 at 17, for a one-under 70 and a four-round score of one-over 284, sole second place. For a golfer who was coming off three poor years brought about by illness and injuries since winning the 2009 Players, the result was reassuring.

"Very happy with my performance," said Stenson. "We're getting closer. I've got two thirds and a second in The Open. We all know what we're longing for."

The first place was taken by Phil Mickelson, who was three ahead of Stenson with two holes remaining. When Stenson birdied 17 to get within two, he told his caddie at 18, "Maybe I can hole my second shot and get into a playoff."

However, Mickelson birdied 18 to achieve the three-stroke lead which would be the final margin.

Known for his wry remarks, Stenson then said to the caddie, "A hole-in-one is pushing it, I think."

—Art Spander

It's a Fact

At age 43 years, 35 days, Phil Mickelson became the oldest Open Champion in 46 years, since Roberto de Vicenzo, who was age 44 years, 92 days, in 1967. The oldest Champion ever was Tom Morris Sr, age 46 years, 102 days in 1867. Mickelson also was the second left-handed player to win The Open, following Sir Bob Charles, who won in 1963 at Royal Lytham and St Annes.

Uncharacteristically, Westwood finished well down the fairways hit and greens in regulation lists (outside the top 65 in both) but topped the putting statistics. "I'm not too disappointed," he said. "I would like to have won but I didn't really feel I was striking the ball well. I was amazed to be in the lead going into the fourth round because every time I turned into the wind I was really struggling."

Stenson, still booming his long irons off the tee to such good effect that no one hit more fairways or greens than the Swede, finished strongly with a birdie at the 17th for an Open runner-up finish to go with two previous third places. The 37-year-old could yet be the first male Swede to win a Major. "Some other time I hope to finish as strongly as Phil did," he said. "I know I can do better with my game, but I can't be disappointed with the performance."

Mickelson's run for glory started with a 5-iron at the 13th which finished 10 feet from the hole. "It was a putt that was going to make the rest of the round go one way or the other," he said. "I thought if I made it, it would give me some momentum because it was very hard to make birdies out there." Yet a 20-footer went in on the 14th and now at one under he was in the thick of it.

He could have come unstuck at the 16th, where his 6-iron tee shot ran up towards the hole and then rolled back down the slope off the front of the green. His chip went seven feet past but he holed that one back for a vital par.

American Harris English finished tied for 15th in his second Open.

Danny Willett posted six over par.

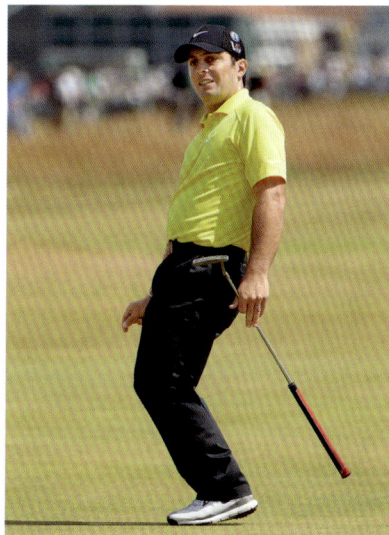
Francesco Molinari had a top-10 finish.

Bo Van Pelt came in with an early 68 for his best score of the week.

Excerpts
FROM THE Press

"They were already evacuating the hospitality suites by the time Tiger Woods made the long walk up the 17th fairway. Those who could, were scrambling over the bank to watch Phil Mickelson. While Lefty cracked open the champagne, Woods was once more left to clear up the empties."

—Jonathan Liew, *The Daily Telegraph*

"For several years, it seemed as if time and life had worn down Phil Mickelson's enthusiasm for tournament golf. Even he admitted occasionally struggling with maintaining concentration over 72 holes. In those months of indifference, it seemed as if the only two things that motivated Mickelson were winning Major Championships and beating Tiger Woods. He got to do both on Sunday at Muirfield in the 142nd Open and now, as they say here, he's the Champion Golfer of the Year."

—Ron Sirak, *Golf Digest.com*

"As he wrapped up his practice session Sunday and started his march to the first tee, Phil Mickelson had a chat with his coach, Butch Harmon, who told his star pupil that even par or lower could win the 142nd edition of the oldest championship in golf. 'I'm going to be better than that,' Mickelson told Harmon despite the fresh breeze blowing in from the nearby hay fields and the Firth of Forth. 'He wasn't lying,' Harmon said."

—Steve DiMeglio, *USA Today*

Mickelson hit two of his best ever 3-woods to reach the 17th green.

"Walking up 17 was the moment I had to compose myself," Mickelson recalled. "I hit two of the best 3-woods I've ever hit and that's exactly why I don't have a driver in the bag. Those two 3-woods were the best shots of the week and walking onto the green I realised this Championship was very much in my control." With others dropping shots behind him, Mickelson was now in sole possession of the lead, a fact he knew thanks to the LED leaderboard by the green. "I believe it is the first year we've had electric scoreboards here at The Open and I was able to see one right there on 17. I knew I was leading and had a chance to get a two-shot lead if I were to two-putt."

When he also birdied the last, Mickelson had completed a thrust that no one else was able to parry. They had not even seen it coming. "I didn't really know what exactly was going on," said Scott. "I wasn't watching the boards so much, but when I looked a couple of times, they didn't seem to make much sense. I wasn't sure if they had it right. Phil kept moving up."

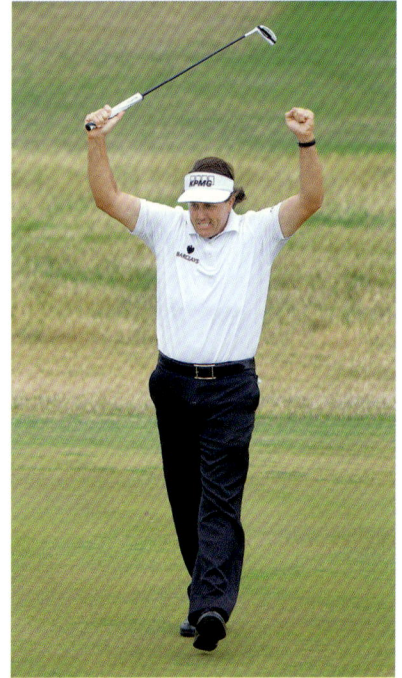

Mickelson holed from 12 feet on the final green and celebrated a famous, and long sought after, victory.

"That was a bit sneaky of him," said Stenson. "I thought I was one or two back, but all of a sudden I was three back. We know Phil is a world-class player, so I don't think it took us by surprise, but all credit to him for finishing the way he did. He's a very worthy Champion after that finish."

"Did anyone else do it today? One guy did it?" Scott added. "We know he goes for broke, and if that's how he's feeling, he's got the ability to pull it off. He's gone and won an Open easily, it looks now."

Mickelson's triumph came just a month after a devastating loss at the US Open at Merion, where he finished as a runner-up for the sixth time. "It's a huge difference in emotions, as you can imagine," he said. "Being so down after the US Open, to come back and use it as motivation, as a springboard, knowing I was playing well, pushed me to work extra hard. You have to be resilient in this game because losing is such a part of it."

Lefty, as he is known, now has three legs of the career Grand Slam under his belt. "I think that is the sign of a complete great player and I'm a leg away," he said. "It's been a tough leg for me. And yet this Championship has been much harder for me to get."

Until Muirfield, 2013, when once again the bold and straight were rewarded, and the timid, gutless and wayward severely punished.

MISSING MAJORS

Five players have achieved the career Grand Slam of winning the Masters, the US Open, The Open Championship and the US PGA Championship: Gene Sarazen, Ben Hogan, Gary Player, Jack Nicklaus and Tiger Woods. Phil Mickelson is the 10th player to win three of the four (missing Major in brackets): Walter Hagen (Masters), Jim Barnes (Masters), Tommy Armour (Masters), Byron Nelson (The Open), Sam Snead (US Open), Arnold Palmer (US PGA), Lee Trevino (Masters), Tom Watson (US PGA), Ray Floyd (The Open), Phil Mickelson (US Open). Hagen, Barnes and Armour only played in the Masters towards the end of their careers. Palmer was a runner-up three times at the US PGA, Snead was a runner-up four times at the US Open, but none of them have gotten closer to a career Grand Slam than Mickelson with six runner-up finishes at the US Open.

MICKELSON FINDS THE SECRET

By John Hopkins

He talked and talked, his eyes darting happily towards each of his questioners. With a wide smile plastered on his face, he made a joke about his Scottishness, or rather his lack of it. For 20 minutes, at least, he held court speaking with vigour, enthusiasm and grace. And for all that time his right hand never left The Open trophy that was placed just in front of him. Not once, not even for a second. "It feels good," Phil Mickelson said.

Little wonder it felt good. He had scarcely got close to it before. Starting in 1991, he had played in The Open every year since, except three. Victory therefore came on his 20th appearance as it had for Darren Clarke in 2011, and no one has waited longer for victory in the game's oldest Major Championship. Mickelson wasn't going to let go of the trophy now.

There were years when he thought he would never win it. He couldn't hit his shots low enough, hard as he tried. He had a magnificent gift for chipping yet he couldn't quite get the hang of the bump and run. And he often seemed frail on the undulating putting surfaces of links courses in England and Scotland where his "hard-at-the-hole" approach didn't bring the same rewards as it would on other greens.

"The common thread is on the greens," Mickelson said when, on the eve of The Open, he was discussing his lack of success on links courses. "I've not putted these greens well. They have subtle nuances and rolls with crosswinds that come into play and strong blades of fescue grass."

Despite being the second best player in the world for some of this time and one of the half dozen best for all this time, Mickelson found links golf to be as great a mystery to him as cricket. In his first 11 appearances he didn't have a single top-10 finish. An exceptional performance at Royal Troon in 2004 where he finished third was followed by five more appearances in which his best finish was tied 19th. In 2011, he said he played some of the best golf of his life on his outward nine holes in the fourth round. The result? A second place behind Clarke. Close but no cigar. You could imagine him climbing on a plane home to California after each Open, and sighing: "It got me again. That links golf is as easy to read as Sanskrit."

But then he and Dave Pelz, his short game coach, found something that would help Mickelson on all greens, not just links, and Mickelson won the Aberdeen Asset Management Scottish Open at Castle Stuart the week before The Open. He arrived on the first tee on a blustery final day with a smile on his face and his hand outstretched to all comers. "Hi, I'm Phil," he said, a statement of the bloomin' obvious.

He began the day two strokes behind Henrik Stenson and hit a scratchy low hook that barely reached the fairway from the first tee and hit a similar tee shot on the second. Soon he was four behind the Swede, only to work his way back first to level, then into the lead and finally despatching Branden Grace with a Mickelsonian chip-and-putt on the first extra hole of a playoff.

"I putted great last week," Mickelson said at Muirfield a couple of days later. "More than that, I've been putting well now for months. I feel like I've really keyed in on something over the past three or four years. You've seen me try the belly putter, you've seen me try different grips. Finally I believe I have found the secret to my own putting and what I need to do to putt well."

Mickelson, asked what the putting secret was while holding on to The Open Championship Trophy, understandably refused to elaborate. Suffice to say that his devastating rush for the line, during which he shouldered all his rivals out of the way, was founded on crisp and accurate iron play and excellent putting. His four birdies in his last six holes in an inward half of 32 that equalled the day's best were down to putts of 10 and 20 feet on the 13th and 14th, seven feet for par on the 16th and 12 feet on the 18th. He didn't so much win The Open as reach out and grab it with both hands. Before he could actually touch it though, there was a tearful scene with Jim "Bones" Mackay, his long-time caddie on the 72nd green. He and Bones hugged one another and through his tears Mickelson whispered: "I did it. I did it."

So there he sat an hour later continuing to answer questions after his triumph. He knew he deserved the trophy and those who were peppering him with questions knew he deserved it, too. He had travelled to Britain year after year, found himself experiencing the full might of Tiger Woods at his best and then serious illnesses to his mother, his wife and himself and he had come through all that.

Just past his 43rd birthday and still holding the silver trophy, he had that enviable look of happiness and contentment on his face. A circle had been squared.

The 142nd Open Championship

Complete Scores

HOLE			1	2	3	4	5	6	7	8	9	10	11	12	13	14	15	16	17	18	
PAR	POSITION		4	4	4	3	5	4	3	4	5	4	4	4	3	4	4	3	5	4	TOTAL
Phil Mickelson	T9	Round 1	4	3	3	3	5	4	3	5	5	4	4	4	3	3	3	3	5	5	69
USA	T11	Round 2	4	6	4	2	5	5	3	4	4	5	3	4	3	4	4	5	5	4	74
£945,000	T9	Round 3	4	3	4	3	6	4	3	4	4	4	4	3	4	4	5	4	5	4	72
	1	Round 4	4	4	4	3	4	4	3	4	4	5	4	4	2	3	4	3	4	3	**66 -281**
Henrik Stenson	T15	Round 1	4	4	5	3	4	4	3	4	5	3	4	4	3	5	4	3	4	4	70
Sweden	T2	Round 2	3	4	4	3	5	6	2	4	4	5	3	4	3	4	5	3	4	4	70
£545,000	T5	Round 3	5	3	4	4	5	5	3	4	5	4	4	4	3	4	4	3	5	5	74
	2	Round 4	3	4	3	3	5	4	3	5	4	4	4	4	5	4	4	3	4	4	**70 -284**
Ian Poulter	T27	Round 1	5	4	3	3	5	4	2	4	4	4	4	4	3	5	5	4	4	5	72
England	T11	Round 2	5	3	4	3	5	5	3	4	4	4	4	4	3	4	4	3	5	4	71
£280,833	T19	Round 3	4	4	4	4	5	5	3	5	4	4	4	4	3	4	4	5	5	5	75
	T3	Round 4	4	4	5	3	4	4	3	4	3	3	3	3	3	4	4	4	5	4	**67 -285**
Adam Scott	T21	Round 1	4	5	4	4	4	4	3	3	5	5	3	4	4	4	4	3	4	5	71
Australia	T11	Round 2	4	4	4	5	5	5	3	4	5	4	4	4	3	4	4	3	4	4	72
£280,833	4	Round 3	4	4	3	4	5	4	3	4	5	4	4	2	4	4	3	5	4		70
	T3	Round 4	5	4	4	4	5	4	2	3	4	4	3	4	4	5	5	4	5	3	**72 -285**
Lee Westwood	T27	Round 1	3	4	4	3	4	4	4	4	6	4	5	4	3	4	5	3	4	4	72
England	T2	Round 2	3	3	4	3	4	4	3	3	4	4	4	3	4	5	4	3	5	5	68
£280,833	1	Round 3	4	4	5	3	3	4	2	5	6	4	4	4	3	3	4	4	4	4	70
	T3	Round 4	4	4	5	3	4	4	4	5	5	4	4	4	4	4	4	4	5	4	**75 -285**
Hideki Matsuyama	T21	Round 1	4	3	4	4	4	4	3	5	5	4	4	5	2	4	5	4	4	3	71
Japan	T20	Round 2	4	4	5	3	5	4	3	5	4	5	4	4	2	5	5	3	4	4	73
£163,333	T11	Round 3	4	4	4	3	5	4	3	4	4	3	4	4	5	4	4	3	6	5	72
	T6	Round 4	4	4	4	3	4	4	3	5	5	4	4	4	2	4	4	3	5	4	**70 -286**
Zach Johnson	1	Round 1	4	4	3	3	3	3	2	4	5	4	4	3	3	5	4	3	5	4	66
USA	T6	Round 2	5	4	4	2	6	5	3	5	4	4	4	3	2	5	6	3	5	5	75
£163,333	T5	Round 3	4	4	4	3	5	4	3	5	5	4	4	4	3	4	4	3	5	4	73
	T6	Round 4	4	4	4	3	5	4	3	4	5	4	3	4	3	5	4	4	5	4	**72 -286**
Tiger Woods	T9	Round 1	5	4	4	2	5	5	3	4	5	3	3	4	2	5	4	3	4	4	69
USA	T2	Round 2	4	4	3	4	4	4	3	5	5	4	5	4	3	4	4	3	5	3	71
£163,333	T2	Round 3	4	3	4	4	5	4	4	4	4	4	4	4	3	4	4	3	6	4	72
	T6	Round 4	5	4	4	4	5	5	3	4	4	5	5	3	3	3	5	3	5	4	**73 -286**

* Denotes amateurs

Player	POSITION	Round	1	2	3	4	5	6	7	8	9	10	11	12	13	14	15	16	17	18	TOTAL
PAR			4	4	4	3	5	4	3	4	5	4	4	4	3	4	4	3	5	4	
Francesco Molinari Italy £115,000	T9	Round 1	5	5	3	2	4	4	4	4	5	4	4	4	3	3	4	3	4	4	69
	T11	Round 2	4	4	4	3	5	5	3	4	5	4	4	4	5	4	4	3	5	4	74
	T9	Round 3	4	5	5	4	5	4	3	3	4	5	4	4	2	4	3	3	6	4	72
	T9	Round 4	4	4	4	3	5	5	3	5	4	4	4	5	2	3	5	3	5	4	72 -287
Hunter Mahan USA £115,000	T27	Round 1	4	4	4	2	4	4	3	4	6	5	4	4	2	4	5	4	5	4	72
	T20	Round 2	4	5	5	2	4	4	3	4	4	4	3	4	4	5	3	5	5	4	72
	T2	Round 3	3	3	4	4	5	4	3	4	4	4	4	4	4	3	3	4	4	4	68
	T9	Round 4	4	5	4	4	5	5	3	4	3	5	4	5	3	4	4	3	5	5	75 -287
Brandt Snedeker USA £93,500	T4	Round 1	4	4	3	3	4	6	4	4	4	4	4	3	3	4	3	3	4	4	68
	T39	Round 2	4	4	3	5	5	4	3	4	4	6	4	3	4	5	7	3	5	6	79
	T11	Round 3	5	4	4	4	4	3	3	4	3	4	5	3	3	4	5	3	5	3	69
	T11	Round 4	4	4	4	4	4	4	3	4	4	5	4	5	3	4	3	3	5	5	72 -288
Angel Cabrera Argentina £93,500	T9	Round 1	5	4	4	3	4	3	3	3	5	4	3	4	3	5	4	3	4	5	69
	T6	Round 2	4	4	4	2	4	5	3	4	4	4	4	4	3	5	5	3	5	5	72
	T5	Round 3	4	4	4	3	5	4	3	4	5	4	4	4	3	4	5	4	5	4	73
	T11	Round 4	5	4	4	3	5	4	3	4	4	5	4	4	4	4	5	3	5	4	74 -288
Justin Leonard USA £79,500	T59	Round 1	5	4	3	3	5	5	2	4	6	5	3	4	4	4	4	4	5	4	74
	T20	Round 2	4	3	4	4	6	4	3	4	4	4	4	4	3	4	3	3	4	5	70
	T19	Round 3	4	4	4	2	5	5	3	4	4	4	4	4	3	5	4	4	6	5	74
	T13	Round 4	5	3	4	4	5	5	3	5	4	4	5	3	3	4	4	3	4	3	71 -289
Miguel A Jimenez Spain £79,500	T4	Round 1	3	3	3	3	4	4	3	4	4	4	4	5	3	4	4	4	5	4	68
	1	Round 2	4	3	4	4	5	4	3	4	5	4	3	4	3	5	4	3	5	4	71
	T11	Round 3	4	5	4	3	6	5	3	5	4	4	4	4	2	5	4	5	6	4	77
	T13	Round 4	4	5	4	3	5	5	3	4	5	4	5	4	3	4	3	5	5	3	73 -289
Eduardo De La Riva Spain £62,250	T47	Round 1	5	4	4	3	6	4	4	4	5	3	4	3	3	5	3	3	5	4	73
	T34	Round 2	4	4	4	4	5	5	3	5	5	4	4	4	3	3	4	3	5	4	73
	T46	Round 3	4	4	5	3	5	4	3	5	4	4	5	4	4	4	5	3	5	4	75
	T15	Round 4	4	4	4	3	6	4	3	4	3	4	4	4	3	4	4	2	5	4	69 -290
Harris English USA £62,250	T59	Round 1	6	4	5	3	4	3	4	4	4	3	5	4	3	3	4	3	5	7	74
	T24	Round 2	3	5	3	3	4	5	3	5	4	4	4	4	3	4	5	4	5	3	71
	T34	Round 3	4	4	5	5	4	4	3	5	4	4	3	5	4	4	4	4	5	4	75
	T15	Round 4	4	3	4	3	6	4	3	4	5	4	4	4	4	4	3	4	4	3	70 -290
Charl Schwartzel South Africa £62,250	T77	Round 1	6	4	4	2	4	4	3	4	5	5	3	5	4	5	6	3	5	3	75
	T11	Round 2	4	3	4	3	4	4	3	4	4	4	4	4	3	3	4	4	5	4	68
	T25	Round 3	5	3	4	5	6	5	4	4	5	5	3	4	3	4	3	4	5	4	76
	T15	Round 4	4	5	3	3	4	5	3	4	5	4	4	4	4	3	3	4	5	5	71 -290
Daniel Willett England £62,250	T77	Round 1	6	4	3	3	4	5	2	4	5	5	4	4	2	5	4	3	6	6	75
	T39	Round 2	4	5	4	3	5	4	3	4	4	5	4	4	3	4	4	2	5	5	72
	T25	Round 3	3	4	4	4	6	6	3	4	4	4	5	3	2	4	4	3	5	4	72
	T15	Round 4	4	4	5	3	4	4	3	4	4	4	4	4	4	4	4	3	5	4	71 -290
Matt Kuchar USA £62,250	T59	Round 1	4	4	5	4	4	5	5	4	4	4	4	4	3	5	4	3	4	4	74
	T39	Round 2	4	4	4	3	5	4	3	4	4	4	4	4	4	4	5	3	5	5	73
	T25	Round 3	4	4	3	3	5	5	3	3	4	5	5	4	3	4	4	4	5	4	72
	T15	Round 4	4	4	5	4	5	4	3	4	4	4	3	4	3	5	4	3	4	4	71 -290
Keegan Bradley USA £62,250	T77	Round 1	6	4	4	3	4	4	3	4	5	4	5	4	3	5	5	4	3	5	75
	T58	Round 2	4	5	4	2	5	4	3	4	5	5	5	4	3	4	4	4	6	3	74
	T25	Round 3	4	4	4	3	4	4	3	4	4	4	4	4	3	4	5	3	5	4	70
	T15	Round 4	4	4	4	3	4	6	3	4	4	4	5	3	3	4	4	3	5	4	71 -290

HOLE			1	2	3	4	5	6	7	8	9	10	11	12	13	14	15	16	17	18	
PAR	POSITION		4	4	4	3	5	4	3	4	5	4	4	4	3	4	4	3	5	4	TOTAL
Stephen Gallacher	T92	Round 1	5	3	4	4	6	5	3	4	6	3	4	5	3	4	4	3	5	5	76
Scotland	T34	Round 2	4	4	4	3	6	4	3	4	3	4	4	4	3	4	4	3	5	4	70
£47,300	T51	Round 3	4	4	4	3	6	3	3	4	5	4	4	3	4	5	5	3	6	6	76
	T21	Round 4	4	4	4	3	5	4	3	4	5	5	4	3	3	4	4	2	4	4	69 -291
Darren Clarke	T27	Round 1	5	4	3	3	5	3	4	4	5	4	3	4	3	5	5	3	4	5	72
Northern Ireland	T11	Round 2	4	4	3	2	4	8	3	4	4	4	4	3	3	4	4	3	5	5	71
£47,300	T25	Round 3	4	4	4	3	6	4	3	4	5	4	4	4	4	6	5	3	5	4	76
	T21	Round 4	4	4	4	3	6	4	2	3	4	5	4	3	3	5	4	3	6	5	72 -291
Richard Sterne	T77	Round 1	4	4	4	3	6	4	3	4	5	4	4	5	4	3	4	3	6	5	75
South Africa	T70	Round 2	4	4	3	4	5	4	3	5	4	5	4	5	2	4	5	4	5	5	75
£47,300	T19	Round 3	4	4	4	4	4	4	2	4	5	4	4	4	2	4	4	3	4	4	68
	T21	Round 4	4	4	4	4	6	4	2	4	6	4	5	3	3	4	4	3	5	4	73 -291
Rafael Cabrera-Bello	T2	Round 1	4	3	4	2	4	4	3	4	6	4	3	4	2	4	5	3	4	4	67
	T6	Round 2	4	4	4	4	4	4	2	5	5	4	5	4	3	6	4	3	4	5	74
Spain	18	Round 3	5	4	5	3	4	4	3	4	4	4	4	5	4	5	4	4	5	5	76
£47,300	**T21**	Round 4	4	4	3	3	6	4	4	5	4	4	4	4	4	5	4	3	5	4	74 -291
Sergio Garcia	T77	Round 1	4	4	3	3	5	3	3	5	4	4	4	5	3	5	4	3	6	5	75
Spain	T49	Round 2	4	4	4	3	4	4	3	5	4	4	4	4	3	4	5	3	6	5	73
£47,300	T11	Round 3	4	3	4	3	5	3	3	5	4	3	5	3	4	4	4	3	5	3	68
	T21	Round 4	5	5	4	3	5	4	3	4	5	4	4	4	4	3	4	3	6	5	75 -291
Jason Dufner	T27	Round 1	4	4	4	4	5	4	3	4	4	4	4	4	5	5	3	3	4	4	72
USA	T58	Round 2	4	5	4	4	4	5	3	4	4	5	4	4	4	4	5	3	6	5	77
£37,250	T74	Round 3	4	4	5	3	5	4	2	5	5	4	4	6	3	4	4	5	4	5	76
	T26	Round 4	3	3	4	4	3	5	5	5	3	5	5	3	4	4	4	4	4	3	71 -292
Stewart Cink	T27	Round 1	4	3	4	3	4	4	3	4	5	5	4	5	2	5	5	3	5	4	72
USA	T39	Round 2	4	4	3	4	4	5	3	4	5	6	4	4	4	5	4	3	5	4	75
£37,250	T63	Round 3	4	4	6	4	6	4	2	4	4	4	4	4	4	4	5	4	5	4	76
	T26	Round 4	3	4	4	3	3	4	2	4	5	5	4	4	3	5	4	4	4	4	69 -292
Jonas Blixt	T27	Round 1	4	3	4	3	5	4	3	6	4	4	4	4	3	4	5	3	5	4	72
Sweden	T70	Round 2	5	3	5	3	6	4	5	5	4	4	5	3	3	5	4	4	5	5	78
£37,250	T63	Round 3	4	4	4	3	4	4	3	5	5	4	4	3	3	5	5	3	5	5	73
	T26	Round 4	6	3	3	3	5	4	3	3	4	4	4	4	2	4	4	4	5	4	69 -292
Steven Tiley	T27	Round 1	4	3	3	3	4	4	4	3	6	4	4	4	3	6	4	3	4	6	72
England	T39	Round 2	4	4	4	3	5	4	3	4	6	5	4	3	3	5	5	3	7	3	75
£37,250	T34	Round 3	4	4	4	3	5	4	3	5	4	5	4	3	4	3	4	6	4	4	73
	T26	Round 4	4	4	4	3	5	5	3	3	6	4	4	4	2	6	4	3	5	3	72 -292
Paul Lawrie	149	Round 1	6	4	4	3	4	4	7	5	5	4	5	5	3	5	5	3	5	4	81
Scotland	T70	Round 2	5	4	3	3	4	5	2	4	4	4	4	3	3	4	4	4	5	4	69
£37,250	T34	Round 3	5	4	4	3	5	4	2	5	4	4	3	3	4	3	5	3	5	4	70
	T26	Round 4	3	4	3	3	6	5	3	6	3	4	4	4	3	5	4	3	5	4	72 -292
Ernie Els	T59	Round 1	5	4	4	3	5	4	3	5	4	4	3	4	3	4	4	6	4	5	74
South Africa	T49	Round 2	4	3	5	3	5	5	3	4	5	5	4	3	3	4	4	3	6	5	74
£37,250	T19	Round 3	4	4	4	3	4	5	4	4	4	5	4	3	2	4	4	3	5	4	70
	T26	Round 4	4	5	3	4	5	4	4	5	4	5	4	4	4	4	5	3	3	4	74 -292
Oliver Fisher	T15	Round 1	4	3	3	3	4	5	3	5	4	4	3	4	5	4	5	3	4	4	70
England	T49	Round 2	5	3	5	4	4	5	3	6	4	5	4	4	4	4	5	4	5	4	78
£25,708	T74	Round 3	5	5	4	4	4	4	3	5	6	3	4	3	3	3	4	4	5	8	77
	T32	Round 4	4	4	3	3	5	4	2	4	4	3	4	5	3	4	4	3	5	4	68 -293

HOLE			1	2	3	4	5	6	7	8	9	10	11	12	13	14	15	16	17	18	
PAR	POSITION		4	4	4	3	5	4	3	4	5	4	4	4	3	4	4	3	5	4	TOTAL
Shane Lowry	T59	Round 1	5	4	3	3	5	4	3	3	6	4	4	4	3	5	5	4	5	4	74
Republic of Ireland	T49	Round 2	4	4	4	4	5	4	3	4	5	4	4	4	3	5	5	4	5	3	74
£25,708	T63	Round 3	4	3	5	3	5	6	3	4	5	4	4	5	3	4	4	3	6	4	75
	T32	Round 4	3	4	4	3	5	4	3	4	3	4	4	4	3	6	4	4	4	4	70 **-293**
Fred Couples	T77	Round 1	4	4	5	2	4	5	5	5	4	4	4	5	3	4	6	3	3	5	75
USA	T58	Round 2	4	4	4	4	4	4	3	5	5	4	5	3	3	5	4	3	5	5	74
£25,708	T51	Round 3	4	4	4	3	6	4	4	4	4	5	5	4	3	3	4	3	4	5	73
	T32	Round 4	4	4	4	4	5	3	2	4	4	4	4	4	2	5	4	3	7	4	71 **-293**
YE Yang	T119	Round 1	6	4	3	3	4	4	3	5	7	5	8	3	2	4	5	3	5	4	78
Korea	T49	Round 2	5	3	4	2	4	4	2	4	5	5	4	4	3	4	5	3	4	5	70
£25,708	T46	Round 3	4	4	5	3	5	4	2	5	5	4	4	4	3	5	3	5	4	4	73
	T32	Round 4	5	4	4	3	4	4	3	4	4	5	4	4	3	4	4	4	5	4	72 **-293**
Thongchai Jaidee	T134	Round 1	5	3	4	3	4	4	4	4	8	4	4	5	6	4	4	3	5	5	79
Thailand	T70	Round 2	4	5	3	4	4	5	3	4	4	3	4	4	3	4	5	3	5	4	71
£25,708	T46	Round 3	4	4	4	3	5	5	2	4	5	3	4	4	3	4	5	3	5	4	71
	T32	Round 4	4	4	4	4	4	5	3	3	5	4	4	4	3	4	4	4	4	5	72 **-293**
Bubba Watson	T15	Round 1	4	5	4	3	5	4	2	4	5	5	4	3	2	4	5	4	3	4	70
USA	T11	Round 2	4	5	3	3	4	4	3	5	4	6	5	3	3	4	4	4	5	4	73
£25,708	T34	Round 3	4	4	4	4	4	4	4	5	5	4	4	4	3	5	5	5	5	4	77
	T32	Round 4	4	4	5	3	4	5	3	4	4	6	4	3	3	4	5	3	5	4	73 **-293**
Bud Cauley	T73	Round 1	7	3	3	4	4	5	3	4	5	5	3	5	2	5	4	2	4	6	74
USA	T58	Round 2	5	5	4	4	5	4	3	5	4	4	4	4	3	5	4	3	5	4	75
£25,708	T34	Round 3	4	4	4	4	4	6	3	4	3	4	4	3	4	4	4	3	5	4	71
	T32	Round 4	3	4	4	3	5	4	2	5	4	5	5	4	3	4	4	4	5	5	73 **-293**
Martin Kaymer	T27	Round 1	4	4	4	3	4	3	4	3	4	6	4	4	4	4	5	4	4	4	72
Germany	T34	Round 2	4	4	5	3	5	5	2	5	4	5	5	3	3	4	5	3	6	3	74
£25,708	T19	Round 3	4	4	4	4	5	6	3	3	5	5	4	4	2	3	4	3	5	4	72
	T32	Round 4	4	4	4	4	7	4	2	4	4	5	5	3	3	5	4	4	5	4	75 **-293**
Dustin Johnson	T4	Round 1	3	4	4	3	4	4	3	3	4	4	4	5	3	4	5	4	3	4	68
USA	T2	Round 2	5	4	4	4	3	5	3	5	4	4	4	3	3	4	5	3	5	4	72
£25,708	T11	Round 3	4	4	4	5	5	5	4	5	4	5	3	4	2	5	4	4	5	4	76
	T32	Round 4	4	4	6	4	5	5	3	5	6	4	4	4	3	4	5	3	4	4	77 **-293**
Jason Day	T47	Round 1	6	4	4	3	4	4	3	3	5	4	4	4	2	4	4	4	5	6	73
Australia	T20	Round 2	4	3	5	4	5	4	2	4	4	5	4	4	2	5	5	3	4	4	71
£25,708	T11	Round 3	4	5	3	3	5	5	3	4	4	4	4	4	3	4	4	4	5	4	71
	T32	Round 4	4	4	4	4	5	4	3	4	6	4	4	7	3	4	4	3	6	4	77 **-293**
Jamie Donaldson	T59	Round 1	4	3	4	3	6	5	4	4	3	4	5	5	4	4	3	3	5	4	74
Wales	T24	Round 2	4	3	5	3	5	4	3	4	4	4	4	4	3	3	5	4	5	4	71
£25,708	T11	Round 3	4	4	4	4	4	4	3	4	5	5	4	4	3	3	4	3	5	4	71
	T32	Round 4	4	4	4	6	5	5	3	5	7	4	4	3	4	3	4	4	3	5	77 **-293**
Ryan Moore	T27	Round 1	3	4	4	4	4	4	3	4	4	6	4	4	3	4	4	5	4	4	72
USA	10	Round 2	4	3	4	3	4	5	3	5	3	4	4	3	3	4	5	3	6	4	70
£25,708	T5	Round 3	4	4	4	4	5	5	4	4	4	3	5	4	2	3	4	3	6	4	72
	T32	Round 4	4	5	5	3	5	5	3	6	4	5	4	4	3	5	4	3	6	5	79 **-293**
Bo Van Pelt	T92	Round 1	4	5	4	3	5	4	5	3	6	6	4	4	3	4	5	3	4	4	76
USA	T58	Round 2	4	4	4	3	5	4	3	4	5	3	6	3	5	5	4	3	4	4	73
£16,139	T79	Round 3	6	4	4	2	5	4	3	5	4	5	5	4	3	5	4	4	5	5	77
	T44	Round 4	4	4	4	4	4	4	3	4	5	4	3	3	3	4	4	3	4	4	68 **-294**

HOLE			1	2	3	4	5	6	7	8	9	10	11	12	13	14	15	16	17	18	
PAR	POSITION		4	4	4	3	5	4	3	4	5	4	4	4	3	4	4	3	5	4	TOTAL
Tim Clark	T27	Round 1	4	4	3	4	5	5	3	5	5	5	4	4	3	4	3	3	4	4	72
South Africa	T49	Round 2	4	5	4	4	5	5	3	4	4	4	4	4	3	4	5	4	5	5	76
£16,139	T68	Round 3	4	4	4	4	5	4	3	4	3	5	5	4	4	4	5	3	6	5	76
	T44	Round 4	4	2	3	3	5	5	3	4	4	4	4	4	3	5	5	3	5	4	70 **-294**
Martin Laird	T15	Round 1	5	3	4	2	4	4	3	4	4	5	4	4	4	5	4	3	4	4	70
Scotland	T6	Round 2	4	5	4	3	4	5	4	4	4	3	3	3	3	5	4	3	6	4	71
£16,139	T51	Round 3	4	3	9	3	4	5	3	5	5	6	4	4	3	4	4	4	7	4	81
	T44	Round 4	4	4	4	3	4	4	3	4	5	5	4	3	4	4	4	4	5	4	72 **-294**
Fredrik Jacobson	T27	Round 1	3	4	3	4	4	5	3	5	5	4	4	4	2	5	4	3	4	6	72
Sweden	T39	Round 2	5	4	4	3	6	5	3	4	4	4	4	4	3	5	4	4	5	4	75
£16,139	T51	Round 3	4	5	5	4	4	5	2	4	4	4	4	5	4	4	4	4	5	4	75
	T44	Round 4	4	4	4	4	4	5	3	4	6	4	4	4	3	4	3	4	4	4	72 **-294**
Matthew Fitzpatrick*	T47	Round 1	4	3	4	3	4	4	3	4	5	5	4	4	3	5	5	3	4	6	73
England	T58	Round 2	4	4	4	3	5	5	4	5	4	4	4	4	3	4	4	3	7	5	76
	T51	Round 3	4	3	4	4	5	4	3	4	4	4	4	5	3	4	4	3	6	5	73
	T44	Round 4	4	4	5	3	5	4	3	4	4	5	4	3	3	6	4	2	5	4	72 **-294**
Geoff Ogilvy	T77	Round 1	4	5	5	3	5	4	3	4	5	4	4	4	4	4	4	4	5	4	75
Australia	T70	Round 2	4	4	5	3	6	4	3	5	4	6	6	4	3	3	3	3	5	4	75
£16,139	T51	Round 3	5	5	4	3	5	6	2	4	6	4	4	4	2	3	3	3	5	4	72
	T44	Round 4	4	4	4	3	4	4	3	4	4	5	5	4	3	5	4	3	5	4	72 **-294**
Mark Brown	T112	Round 1	5	4	4	3	4	5	4	4	4	4	4	7	4	5	5	2	5	4	77
New Zealand	T70	Round 2	5	4	5	3	5	4	4	4	4	3	4	4	3	4	5	2	6	4	73
£16,139	T51	Round 3	4	4	4	4	5	5	3	4	3	4	4	4	3	4	5	3	5	4	72
	T44	Round 4	4	3	3	3	4	4	3	4	5	6	3	5	4	3	4	4	6	4	72 **-294**
KJ Choi	T92	Round 1	4	4	4	4	5	3	3	5	6	6	3	5	3	4	5	3	4	5	76
Korea	T70	Round 2	3	4	5	4	5	4	3	4	4	6	4	4	4	4	5	3	4	4	74
£16,139	T46	Round 3	4	4	5	3	5	4	3	4	4	4	4	4	3	5	4	3	5	3	71
	T44	Round 4	4	4	4	3	4	4	3	5	5	4	4	4	3	4	4	3	6	5	73 **-294**
Jordan Spieth	T9	Round 1	4	4	3	4	4	4	3	4	4	5	4	4	3	4	3	4	4	4	69
USA	T11	Round 2	4	4	4	3	5	4	3	5	4	4	3	4	3	4	6	4	6	4	74
£16,139	T25	Round 3	4	4	5	5	5	3	3	4	4	5	4	5	4	3	4	4	5	5	76
	T44	Round 4	4	4	4	5	5	4	2	4	5	6	4	3	3	5	5	3	5	4	75 **-294**
Shingo Katayama	T47	Round 1	4	4	3	3	5	4	3	5	4	6	6	3	2	4	4	3	5	5	73
Japan	T70	Round 2	5	4	4	3	5	5	4	5	6	3	4	5	3	4	5	3	5	4	77
£16,139	T25	Round 3	4	4	4	3	4	4	2	5	4	4	5	4	3	4	4	2	5	4	69
	T44	Round 4	4	4	4	3	4	5	5	4	5	5	4	3	3	5	4	3	5	5	75 **-294**
Padraig Harrington	T47	Round 1	4	4	4	3	4	4	3	5	4	5	4	4	4	5	4	3	5	4	73
Republic of Ireland	T49	Round 2	4	4	4	3	4	4	4	4	5	5	4	4	3	5	5	4	4	5	75
£13,725	T74	Round 3	4	4	4	4	5	5	3	4	5	5	4	4	4	3	4	5	5	5	77
	T54	Round 4	4	4	4	3	4	4	3	4	4	4	4	4	4	4	4	3	5	4	70 **-295**
Marcus Fraser	T47	Round 1	4	4	4	3	4	4	5	4	5	4	3	4	4	4	4	4	5	4	73
Australia	T39	Round 2	4	3	3	3	6	4	3	4	5	4	3	3	4	4	6	4	6	5	74
£13,725	T63	Round 3	5	5	4	3	5	5	3	5	4	5	4	4	3	4	4	3	5	5	76
	T54	Round 4	5	4	4	3	5	3	3	4	5	4	3	4	3	5	4	3	6	4	72 **-295**
Gonzalo	T15	Round 1	4	4	3	3	6	3	4	5	5	4	4	4	3	4	4	2	4	4	70
Fernandez-Castano	T58	Round 2	5	5	4	3	4	5	3	7	5	4	4	4	3	5	5	3	5	5	79
Spain	T51	Round 3	4	4	4	3	4	5	3	4	5	4	4	4	3	4	4	4	6	4	73
£13,725	**T54**	Round 4	4	4	4	3	4	4	3	4	4	7	4	4	5	4	4	3	5	3	73 **-295**

HOLE			1	2	3	4	5	6	7	8	9	10	11	12	13	14	15	16	17	18	
PAR	POSITION		4	4	4	3	5	4	3	4	5	4	4	4	3	4	4	3	5	4	TOTAL
Carl Pettersson	T59	Round 1	3	4	4	4	5	4	4	4	5	4	4	4	4	5	3	4	5	4	74
Sweden	T70	Round 2	4	5	3	3	5	3	3	5	5	5	6	4	3	5	5	3	5	4	76
£13,725	T34	Round 3	4	5	4	4	5	4	2	3	5	4	4	3	4	3	4	3	5	4	70
	T54	Round 4	4	3	5	4	5	5	3	4	4	4	4	4	3	4	5	3	5	6	75 -295
Mark O'Meara	T2	Round 1	3	3	4	3	4	3	3	4	4	5	4	4	3	5	5	3	3	4	67
USA	T24	Round 2	4	4	5	3	5	6	3	5	5	4	4	3	3	5	4	4	6	5	78
£13,150	T51	Round 3	3	4	4	3	5	5	3	4	5	5	4	5	4	4	5	4	6	4	77
	T58	Round 4	4	4	4	3	5	3	3	5	5	5	5	4	4	4	3	3	5	5	74 -296
Richie Ramsay	T92	Round 1	5	4	3	3	4	5	4	5	4	4	4	4	3	5	4	4	5	6	76
Scotland	T70	Round 2	4	4	3	4	5	4	2	4	5	4	4	4	4	5	5	4	4	5	74
£13,150	T51	Round 3	4	4	3	4	6	3	4	4	5	3	4	4	3	5	4	3	5	4	72
	T58	Round 4	4	4	4	3	5	5	3	4	4	4	4	4	3	4	4	4	5	6	74 -296
Boo Weekley	T59	Round 1	3	5	4	5	4	6	3	5	4	4	4	4	3	4	5	2	5	4	74
USA	T70	Round 2	4	4	4	3	4	4	3	5	5	5	3	4	4	4	6	3	7	4	76
£13,150	T46	Round 3	4	4	6	3	3	4	3	4	5	4	4	4	3	4	4	3	4	5	71
	T58	Round 4	5	4	4	3	4	5	3	5	4	4	4	5	3	4	4	4	6	4	75 -296
Tom Lehman	T4	Round 1	5	3	4	3	4	4	3	5	4	4	4	4	3	4	4	3	4	3	68
USA	T24	Round 2	4	4	4	3	5	5	3	4	5	4	4	5	3	4	6	4	5	5	77
£13,150	T34	Round 3	4	5	5	4	5	5	3	4	4	5	4	4	4	3	4	3	5	4	75
	T58	Round 4	5	4	4	4	4	4	4	5	5	5	4	4	2	4	4	4	5	5	76 -296
Graeme McDowell	T77	Round 1	4	4	4	3	4	5	3	3	7	4	4	4	3	4	6	3	5	5	75
Northern Ireland	T34	Round 2	4	3	4	3	5	4	3	4	4	5	5	4	2	5	4	3	5	4	71
£13,150	T25	Round 3	4	4	5	3	4	5	3	5	6	4	4	3	3	3	4	3	5	5	73
	T58	Round 4	5	6	4	4	5	4	3	5	5	4	4	4	3	4	4	4	5	4	77 -296
Johnson Wagner	T47	Round 1	5	3	4	2	5	5	4	5	5	4	4	4	3	4	5	3	4	4	73
USA	T24	Round 2	4	3	4	3	4	5	3	3	6	5	4	4	3	5	4	3	5	4	72
£13,150	T19	Round 3	3	4	4	3	6	3	3	4	5	5	5	4	3	4	4	4	5	4	73
	T58	Round 4	5	4	4	4	5	4	3	4	5	4	5	4	6	4	4	4	5	4	78 -296
Ben Curtis	T59	Round 1	4	4	4	3	5	4	2	4	5	7	4	4	4	4	4	3	5	4	74
USA	T24	Round 2	4	4	3	3	5	4	3	4	4	4	4	3	3	5	5	4	5	4	71
£12,500	T74	Round 3	5	4	5	5	4	4	2	6	4	4	4	4	5	6	4	3	6	5	80
	T64	Round 4	4	4	5	3	5	4	2	6	5	5	4	3	2	5	3	3	5	4	72 -297
Chris Wood	T77	Round 1	7	4	4	3	5	4	3	4	4	5	3	4	3	6	3	5	4	4	75
England	T70	Round 2	4	4	4	3	4	4	3	6	4	5	3	5	4	5	4	4	5	4	75
£12,500	T74	Round 3	4	4	4	3	4	5	3	4	4	5	4	4	3	5	5	5	5	4	75
	T64	Round 4	4	4	4	3	5	4	3	5	5	5	4	4	3	4	5	2	4	4	72 -297
Branden Grace	T59	Round 1	6	4	4	3	5	4	3	4	5	4	3	4	4	5	4	2	6	4	74
South Africa	T24	Round 2	4	3	4	5	5	4	3	3	5	3	4	4	4	5	4	2	5	4	71
£12,500	T51	Round 3	4	4	3	4	6	4	3	6	4	5	3	4	4	4	4	3	7	5	77
	T64	Round 4	4	5	4	3	5	6	2	4	6	4	4	3	3	5	4	4	5	4	75 -297
Webb Simpson	T47	Round 1	5	5	4	2	4	4	3	5	4	4	4	3	3	5	4	4	5	5	73
USA	T11	Round 2	4	4	3	3	5	5	3	4	4	3	4	4	3	4	5	3	5	4	70
£12,500	T34	Round 3	4	4	4	3	6	4	3	5	5	5	4	4	3	6	4	4	4	5	77
	T64	Round 4	4	4	4	3	6	5	4	5	4	5	5	5	3	4	4	3	5	4	77 -297
Bernd Wiesberger	T21	Round 1	4	3	4	4	4	3	3	5	5	5	4	4	3	4	5	3	5	3	71
Austria	T24	Round 2	4	5	4	5	5	4	3	4	4	3	4	4	3	5	5	2	5	5	74
£12,500	T34	Round 3	4	4	5	4	4	5	3	4	4	4	4	3	3	5	5	3	6	5	75
	T64	Round 4	4	4	4	3	6	6	3	5	4	4	4	4	3	4	6	3	6	4	77 -297

HOLE			1	2	3	4	5	6	7	8	9	10	11	12	13	14	15	16	17	18	
PAR	POSITION		4	4	4	3	5	4	3	4	5	4	4	4	3	4	4	3	5	4	TOTAL
Gregory Bourdy	T92	Round 1	4	4	4	3	4	4	4	7	5	4	4	6	2	4	5	3	5	4	76
France	T34	Round 2	4	4	4	3	5	4	3	4	4	4	4	3	3	4	4	4	5	4	70
£12,500	T34	Round 3	4	4	5	4	6	5	2	4	4	4	4	3	4	4	4	4	5	4	74
	T64	Round 4	4	4	4	4	5	4	3	5	6	4	5	3	3	4	3	5	5	6	77 **-297**
Ken Duke	T15	Round 1	4	4	5	3	4	4	3	4	5	4	4	4	4	4	5	2	3	4	70
USA	T39	Round 2	4	4	4	3	5	5	4	4	5	4	4	4	4	6	3	3	6	5	77
£12,500	T34	Round 3	4	4	5	4	4	4	3	6	4	4	3	4	3	4	5	3	5	4	73
	T64	Round 4	4	3	4	3	5	6	2	4	5	4	6	3	4	5	6	3	5	5	77 **-297**
Gareth Wright	T21	Round 1	5	4	4	3	4	4	2	5	5	4	3	5	3	4	4	3	5	4	71
Wales	T58	Round 2	4	3	4	5	6	5	3	4	4	4	4	5	4	5	5	4	5	4	78
£12,050	T68	Round 3	4	4	4	5	6	5	4	4	4	4	5	3	3	4	4	3	4	5	75
	T71	Round 4	3	3	4	5	6	3	3	4	6	5	4	4	3	4	4	4	5	4	74 **-298**
George Coetzee	T92	Round 1	4	4	4	2	5	5	3	4	5	4	4	5	3	6	4	4	4	6	76
South Africa	T39	Round 2	4	4	4	3	6	4	3	4	4	3	4	5	2	5	4	2	5	5	71
£12,050	T51	Round 3	4	4	4	4	5	5	3	4	4	4	5	4	3	4	4	3	6	5	75
	T71	Round 4	5	4	4	3	4	4	3	5	4	4	5	5	4	4	5	4	5	4	76 **-298**
Shiv Kapur	T4	Round 1	3	3	3	3	4	3	2	4	5	6	4	4	3	5	4	3	5	4	68
India	T24	Round 2	5	4	5	4	5	5	3	4	4	5	4	3	4	4	4	3	6	5	77
£11,700	T83	Round 3	4	4	5	6	6	7	3	4	5	4	4	3	5	5	4	5	5	4	83
	T73	Round 4	4	4	3	3	4	5	3	4	4	5	4	5	3	4	4	3	6	3	71 **-299**
KT Kim	T47	Round 1	3	4	4	3	5	4	3	5	4	6	5	4	4	4	3	3	4	5	73
Korea	T58	Round 2	5	5	4	4	4	5	3	4	4	5	3	4	4	4	4	4	4	6	76
£11,700	T79	Round 3	4	4	4	5	4	4	3	5	5	4	5	4	4	4	6	3	5	4	77
	T73	Round 4	4	3	4	3	4	4	3	5	5	4	3	4	3	4	4	3	7	6	73 **-299**
Russell Henley	T119	Round 1	5	5	4	3	5	4	3	6	6	4	4	4	4	6	4	3	4	4	78
USA	T58	Round 2	5	3	4	3	6	4	3	5	4	4	4	3	4	4	3	4	4	4	71
£11,700	T68	Round 3	4	4	5	3	6	4	3	4	4	4	6	4	2	5	4	4	6	3	75
	T73	Round 4	4	3	5	4	5	4	4	6	5	4	3	4	4	6	3	3	4	4	75 **-299**
Jimmy Mullen*	T21	Round 1	4	3	3	4	4	4	4	3	5	6	5	3	3	4	4	3	4	5	71
England	T58	Round 2	4	4	5	3	6	4	5	5	5	4	3	4	4	6	5	3	5	3	78
	T68	Round 3	5	4	4	4	5	6	3	4	4	5	3	4	3	4	3	4	6	4	75
	T73	Round 4	5	4	3	4	5	5	2	4	7	4	4	4	3	4	4	3	5	5	75 **-299**
Todd Hamilton	T9	Round 1	4	4	4	4	4	4	4	4	4	4	4	4	2	4	4	3	4	4	69
USA	T70	Round 2	5	5	4	3	4	6	4	5	5	4	5	4	3	6	5	3	5	5	81
£11,700	T34	Round 3	4	3	4	3	5	4	3	4	4	4	4	4	3	4	4	3	5	5	70
	T73	Round 4	4	4	4	4	5	5	3	4	5	4	4	5	4	5	4	4	6	5	79 **-299**
Thomas Bjorn	T47	Round 1	6	4	4	4	5	4	2	4	4	4	3	4	3	4	3	4	7	4	73
Denmark	T39	Round 2	4	4	4	3	5	4	3	5	5	5	4	4	3	4	4	3	5	5	74
£11,700	T25	Round 3	3	4	3	5	4	5	3	3	4	4	4	4	4	4	4	4	5	5	72
	T73	Round 4	3	4	3	4	6	5	4	5	6	4	4	5	4	6	4	4	5	4	80 **-299**
Kevin Streelman	T59	Round 1	5	3	3	4	4	5	3	5	5	5	4	5	2	5	4	3	5	4	74
USA	T24	Round 2	4	5	3	3	5	4	3	4	4	4	4	4	3	4	4	4	4	5	71
£11,300	82	Round 3	4	3	6	4	5	5	6	4	6	4	4	4	5	5	5	3	5	4	82
	T79	Round 4	4	4	4	3	4	4	4	4	5	4	5	4	3	5	4	3	5	5	73 **-300**
Mikko Ilonen	T27	Round 1	3	4	3	3	4	7	3	4	4	5	4	5	4	5	3	3	4	4	72
Finland	T70	Round 2	4	4	4	4	6	3	3	5	4	4	5	4	3	5	6	3	6	5	78
£11,300	T79	Round 3	4	4	4	4	5	4	4	4	6	6	4	4	3	4	4	3	5	4	76
	T79	Round 4	4	4	4	3	4	5	4	4	5	4	3	4	5	5	4	3	5	4	74 **-300**

| HOLE | | | 1 | 2 | 3 | 4 | 5 | 6 | 7 | 8 | 9 | 10 | 11 | 12 | 13 | 14 | 15 | 16 | 17 | 18 | |
PAR	POSITION		4	4	4	3	5	4	3	4	5	4	4	4	3	4	4	3	5	4	TOTAL
Peter Senior	T59	Round 1	6	3	4	3	5	4	3	4	5	4	3	4	4	4	5	4	4	5	74
Australia	T70	Round 2	4	4	4	3	6	5	3	5	4	4	4	5	4	4	5	3	4	5	76
£11,300	T63	Round 3	5	4	4	3	5	4	3	5	4	4	3	3	4	5	5	3	5	4	73
	T79	Round 4	5	4	5	4	5	4	3	5	5	4	4	4	3	4	4	3	6	5	77 **-300**
Josh Teater	T27	Round 1	4	4	3	3	6	4	2	5	5	3	4	5	4	4	5	3	4	4	72
USA	T58	Round 2	4	4	5	3	5	4	3	5	5	5	4	4	3	4	5	4	5	5	77
£11,100	T68	Round 3	4	4	4	3	4	4	3	5	5	5	5	4	3	4	4	5	5	4	75
	82	Round 4	4	4	5	4	5	5	3	5	6	4	4	4	3	4	4	3	6	4	77 **-301**
Graham DeLaet	T92	Round 1	5	4	4	3	5	4	3	5	4	6	4	4	3	5	5	3	5	4	76
Canada	T49	Round 2	4	4	5	3	5	5	3	5	4	4	4	3	2	5	3	3	5	4	72
£11,000	T68	Round 3	4	5	4	5	6	4	3	5	6	5	4	4	3	4	4	3	4	3	76
	83	Round 4	6	6	4	4	4	5	3	5	6	4	4	5	3	4	4	3	5	4	79 **-303**
Sandy Lyle	T92	Round 1	4	4	4	3	5	5	3	5	5	5	3	6	4	5	5	2	5	3	76
Scotland	T49	Round 2	5	4	5	3	5	5	4	4	4	3	4	4	4	3	4	3	5	3	72
£10,900	T83	Round 3	4	4	4	4	5	5	3	4	6	4	4	5	5	4	4	5	5	5	80
	84	Round 4	5	4	5	3	5	4	2	4	5	5	4	8	2	4	6	3	6	4	79 **-307**

NON QUALIFIERS AFTER 36 HOLES

(Leading 10 professionals and ties receive £3,700 each, next 20 professionals and ties receive £3,000 each, remainder of professionals receive £2,500 each.)

| HOLE | | | 1 | 2 | 3 | 4 | 5 | 6 | 7 | 8 | 9 | 10 | 11 | 12 | 13 | 14 | 15 | 16 | 17 | 18 | |
PAR	POSITION		4	4	4	3	5	4	3	4	5	4	4	4	3	4	4	3	5	4	TOTAL
Oscar Floren	T59	Round 1	4	4	4	3	5	3	3	4	6	5	4	4	3	5	4	4	5	4	74
Sweden	**T85**	Round 2	4	4	5	4	5	5	3	4	4	4	4	4	4	4	5	4	6	4	77 **-151**
Marc Leishman	T92	Round 1	5	4	5	5	4	4	3	5	5	5	4	4	3	4	4	3	4	5	76
Australia	**T85**	Round 2	5	4	3	3	6	4	3	5	4	5	4	4	4	5	5	3	4	4	75 **-151**
Alvaro Quiros	T112	Round 1	4	5	5	3	4	4	3	4	3	5	6	6	5	5	3	4	3	5	77
Spain	**T85**	Round 2	4	4	4	4	5	6	4	6	4	4	4	3	3	4	4	3	4	4	74 **-151**
Kyle Stanley	T150	Round 1	4	7	4	5	7	5	3	4	7	4	5	4	3	5	4	2	5	4	82
USA	**T85**	Round 2	4	4	3	3	4	4	3	4	5	4	3	4	3	4	5	3	4	5	69 **-151**
Michael Thompson	T27	Round 1	4	4	4	4	4	4	3	3	5	4	3	5	3	5	5	3	4	5	72
USA	**T85**	Round 2	5	4	4	4	5	4	3	5	6	4	4	4	6	4	4	4	5	4	79 **-151**
Bill Haas	T112	Round 1	4	4	4	4	4	3	4	4	6	4	4	5	4	4	5	4	5	5	77
USA	**T85**	Round 2	5	5	4	3	5	4	2	4	4	4	5	4	3	5	5	3	6	3	74 **-151**
Marcel Siem	T77	Round 1	4	4	4	3	5	6	3	4	5	4	4	4	3	5	5	3	4	5	75
Germany	**T85**	Round 2	4	4	5	5	6	5	3	4	3	4	4	4	3	4	4	4	5	5	76 **-151**
George Murray	T92	Round 1	4	4	4	6	5	4	3	4	5	4	4	4	3	4	4	5	4	5	76
Scotland	**T85**	Round 2	4	5	4	4	6	4	2	5	4	4	5	4	4	4	4	3	5	4	75 **-151**
Thomas Aiken	T21	Round 1	5	4	4	3	4	4	2	5	4	5	4	4	3	5	4	2	5	4	71
South Africa	**T85**	Round 2	6	4	6	3	5	4	4	4	4	4	4	4	3	5	5	4	5	6	80 **-151**
Jimmy Walker	T27	Round 1	4	4	3	4	4	4	3	4	4	6	4	4	5	4	4	3	4	4	72
USA	**T85**	Round 2	6	4	4	4	5	5	4	4	4	4	4	4	3	5	5	3	6	5	79 **-151**
Nicolas Colsaerts	T77	Round 1	4	4	4	3	4	5	3	5	4	5	4	4	3	4	6	3	6	4	75
Belgium	**T85**	Round 2	5	4	4	3	5	4	3	5	5	3	4	4	3	4	9	4	4	3	76 **-151**
Camilo Villegas	T27	Round 1	4	4	4	3	5	4	3	4	5	3	4	4	4	4	4	3	5	5	72
Colombia	**T85**	Round 2	5	4	4	3	4	4	4	5	4	5	4	4	5	5	5	3	5	6	79 **-151**

HOLE			1	2	3	4	5	6	7	8	9	10	11	12	13	14	15	16	17	18	
PAR	POSITION		4	4	4	3	5	4	3	4	5	4	4	4	3	4	4	3	5	4	TOTAL
Niclas Fasth	T112	Round 1	4	4	5	3	5	5	4	3	5	4	5	4	3	5	6	3	5	4	77
Sweden	**T97**	Round 2	4	4	4	4	4	5	4	4	5	4	4	3	3	5	5	3	7	3	75 -152
Jim Furyk	T119	Round 1	5	4	4	3	4	4	3	5	5	5	5	5	4	5	4	3	4	6	78
USA	**T97**	Round 2	4	4	4	3	4	5	3	4	5	6	4	4	2	4	4	3	6	5	74 -152
Luke Donald	T143	Round 1	5	4	4	3	6	4	3	5	5	3	4	6	3	7	5	4	4	5	80
England	**T97**	Round 2	3	4	3	3	5	4	3	4	5	5	4	4	3	4	5	4	5	4	72 -152
Hiroyuki Fujita	T119	Round 1	4	4	4	3	6	5	2	5	5	4	4	4	4	4	6	4	5	5	78
Japan	**T97**	Round 2	4	5	4	3	4	4	4	4	5	5	4	4	4	5	3	4	4	4	74 -152
Justin Harding	T119	Round 1	5	3	4	3	4	4	3	6	5	3	5	5	4	5	5	4	6	4	78
South Africa	**T97**	Round 2	4	6	5	4	5	4	3	4	5	4	5	4	3	4	3	3	4	4	74 -152
Stephen Dartnall	T143	Round 1	4	5	4	5	6	4	5	4	5	4	5	4	4	4	4	3	5	5	80
Australia	**T97**	Round 2	5	4	5	3	5	4	4	3	3	5	4	3	3	4	5	3	5	4	72 -152
Marc Warren	T27	Round 1	4	4	4	3	4	5	3	4	5	4	4	4	4	4	4	3	5	4	72
Scotland	**T97**	Round 2	4	4	5	4	5	5	3	5	4	7	4	4	3	4	4	4	5	6	80 -152
Justin Rose	T77	Round 1	4	4	4	3	5	5	3	4	6	4	4	4	3	5	6	3	4	4	75
England	**T97**	Round 2	4	5	4	3	5	6	3	4	4	6	5	4	3	4	4	3	5	5	77 -152
Nick Watney	T77	Round 1	4	3	4	4	3	4	3	4	5	4	4	4	4	5	6	4	5	5	75
USA	**T97**	Round 2	4	4	4	5	5	4	3	3	6	5	4	3	4	4	6	4	5	4	77 -152
Mark Calcavecchia	T27	Round 1	5	4	3	4	5	3	6	5	4	4	4	3	4	3	3	5	3	4	72
USA	**T97**	Round 2	4	5	4	3	5	5	3	5	8	4	4	3	4	5	5	3	6	4	80 -152
Hyung-Sung Kim	T92	Round 1	4	4	3	4	4	4	4	4	4	7	4	4	7	5	4	3	3	4	76
Korea	**T97**	Round 2	5	4	4	3	5	7	4	4	4	4	4	4	2	4	5	3	5	5	76 -152
Toru Taniguchi	T119	Round 1	4	4	5	6	4	4	2	4	6	4	4	4	4	4	5	4	6	4	78
Japan	**T108**	Round 2	4	3	4	3	4	6	3	4	6	4	4	4	4	4	5	3	5	5	75 -153
DA Points	T119	Round 1	5	5	4	4	4	4	2	6	4	5	4	4	5	4	4	3	5	6	78
USA	**T108**	Round 2	4	4	4	5	4	5	3	4	4	4	4	4	4	4	5	3	5	5	75 -153
Ben Stow*	T92	Round 1	4	4	3	3	5	4	4	5	7	4	4	5	3	4	4	4	4	5	76
England	**T108**	Round 2	5	4	4	3	7	6	3	4	4	4	4	3	4	6	3	4	6	3	77 -153
Ashun Wu	T92	Round 1	5	3	4	2	5	4	3	4	6	5	5	5	2	5	5	3	6	4	76
China	**T108**	Round 2	4	5	4	3	5	5	3	5	4	5	4	4	5	5	4	3	5	4	77 -153
Robert Garrigus	T119	Round 1	4	5	4	3	6	4	3	5	5	4	5	3	4	5	4	3	6	5	78
USA	**T108**	Round 2	4	4	4	4	5	4	3	4	6	4	4	5	3	4	2	4	6	5	75 -153
John Senden	T112	Round 1	6	5	5	2	4	4	3	5	6	5	4	4	4	5	3	4	4	4	77
Australia	**T108**	Round 2	4	3	4	3	5	5	3	5	4	6	4	4	4	5	4	4	5	4	76 -153
Garrick Porteous*	T92	Round 1	4	4	3	5	5	4	4	4	6	4	6	5	3	3	4	3	5	4	76
England	**T108**	Round 2	4	4	5	4	5	5	3	4	4	4	4	5	5	4	4	3	5	5	77 -153
Tom Watson	T77	Round 1	5	4	4	4	4	5	2	5	5	5	3	4	3	4	4	4	6	4	75
USA	**T108**	Round 2	4	4	4	3	7	5	5	4	5	4	3	5	4	4	4	3	6	4	78 -153
Vijay Singh	T112	Round 1	5	3	3	4	5	5	5	5	5	5	3	4	4	5	4	4	4	4	77
Fiji	**T116**	Round 2	4	5	5	3	6	5	3	6	4	4	4	4	3	4	4	4	5	4	77 -154
Thorbjorn Olesen	T119	Round 1	5	4	4	4	7	4	3	4	3	5	4	3	5	5	4	3	6	5	78
Denmark	**T116**	Round 2	4	4	5	3	5	4	3	4	4	3	3	4	4	6	4	7	5		76 -154
Rickie Fowler	T119	Round 1	6	4	4	3	4	6	4	5	5	4	4	4	4	4	5	3	4	5	78
USA	**T116**	Round 2	4	3	4	4	5	4	3	7	4	5	4	4	3	4	5	3	5	5	76 -154
Gareth Maybin	T119	Round 1	5	4	6	3	4	4	3	3	7	6	4	5	5	4	4	3	4	4	78
Northern Ireland	**T116**	Round 2	4	5	4	3	5	5	4	5	4	4	4	4	4	4	5	3	5	4	76 -154
Robert Karlsson	T112	Round 1	4	4	3	4	5	4	3	4	6	4	4	5	3	5	5	4	5	5	77
Sweden	**T116**	Round 2	3	5	4	4	5	4	2	4	5	5	6	4	3	4	5	3	5	6	77 -154

HOLE			1	2	3	4	5	6	7	8	9	10	11	12	13	14	15	16	17	18	
PAR	POSITION		4	4	4	3	5	4	3	4	5	4	4	4	3	4	4	3	5	4	TOTAL
Scott Stallings	T92	Round 1	4	5	4	3	5	4	3	5	5	5	4	6	3	4	4	3	5	4	76
USA	**T116**	Round 2	5	4	4	3	6	5	3	6	4	5	4	4	3	4	5	3	5	5	78-**154**
David Lynn	T134	Round 1	5	4	4	4	4	4	5	5	6	5	4	4	4	4	4	5	5	3	79
England	**T116**	Round 2	4	4	4	4	4	5	3	5	5	5	4	4	3	4	4	3	6	4	75-**154**
Billy Horschel	T59	Round 1	5	4	4	3	4	4	4	5	4	4	7	4	3	3	4	3	5	4	74
USA	**T116**	Round 2	4	5	5	3	5	4	3	6	5	5	4	4	3	5	6	3	5	5	80-**154**
Rory McIlroy	T134	Round 1	4	4	4	4	6	4	2	4	5	5	5	6	2	4	6	3	6	5	79
Northern Ireland	**T116**	Round 2	4	4	5	4	5	4	5	5	4	5	4	4	3	5	3	3	4	4	75-**154**
John Huh	T59	Round 1	5	3	4	4	5	4	3	4	5	5	4	4	3	4	5	3	5	4	74
USA	**T116**	Round 2	5	4	4	3	6	4	3	5	5	5	4	4	2	7	4	4	6	5	80-**154**
Kenichi Kuboya	T92	Round 1	4	4	5	4	3	4	4	4	6	5	5	5	2	6	5	3	3	4	76
Japan	**T126**	Round 2	5	4	5	4	5	4	3	5	6	4	5	3	4	4	5	4	5	4	79-**155**
Darryn Lloyd	T134	Round 1	4	4	4	4	6	6	3	5	4	5	5	4	3	5	5	3	6	3	79
South Africa	**T126**	Round 2	4	4	3	4	5	5	3	4	4	4	4	4	3	5	4	3	6	7	76-**155**
David Duval	T92	Round 1	5	3	5	3	5	5	3	6	5	4	4	4	3	4	4	3	5	5	76
USA	**T126**	Round 2	4	4	4	4	6	5	2	6	4	4	4	5	3	5	5	4	6	4	79-**155**
Richard McEvoy	T47	Round 1	5	4	4	3	4	4	2	5	5	5	4	4	4	3	5	3	5	4	73
England	**T126**	Round 2	4	5	4	4	5	4	3	5	6	5	4	4	3	4	6	6	5	5	82-**155**
Steven Jeffress	T92	Round 1	5	3	4	3	5	5	4	4	5	4	5	5	3	4	5	3	5	4	76
Australia	**T126**	Round 2	4	5	4	3	7	4	3	6	4	4	4	4	5	4	4	4	5	5	79-**155**
John Wade	T59	Round 1	4	4	4	3	6	4	4	4	5	4	4	4	3	3	5	4	5	4	74
Australia	**T126**	Round 2	4	5	5	3	5	5	3	5	4	4	4	4	3	8	5	2	5	7	81-**155**
Thaworn Wiratchant	T134	Round 1	5	4	4	3	4	4	3	5	5	5	4	6	4	4	5	3	5	6	79
Thailand	**T132**	Round 2	4	4	4	4	5	4	3	5	5	5	5	4	4	4	3	5	5	4	77-**156**
Lucas Glover	T143	Round 1	4	4	5	3	6	5	3	5	5	5	5	4	3	4	5	4	6	4	80
USA	**T132**	Round 2	5	5	5	3	4	5	2	5	4	4	4	5	3	5	4	4	5	4	76-**156**
Brett Rumford	T134	Round 1	5	4	4	3	4	4	3	5	6	5	5	3	5	4	3	6	5	79	
Australia	**T132**	Round 2	5	4	4	4	4	4	3	5	4	5	4	3	4	5	5	3	6	5	77-**156**
Scott Jamieson	T143	Round 1	4	4	4	3	5	4	4	4	5	5	4	5	3	6	5	6	5	4	80
Scotland	**T132**	Round 2	4	5	4	4	7	6	4	4	5	5	4	3	2	3	5	2	5	4	76-**156**
Lloyd Saltman	T134	Round 1	8	4	3	2	5	4	4	5	6	5	4	4	4	4	4	3	5	4	79
Scotland	**T132**	Round 2	4	4	4	4	5	5	3	5	4	4	4	5	4	5	5	2	6	4	77-**156**
Brooks Koepka	T92	Round 1	8	4	3	3	3	4	3	4	6	4	4	5	3	5	4	3	5	5	76
USA	**T132**	Round 2	4	4	4	4	6	4	3	5	5	5	4	3	4	5	5	4	5	6	80-**156**
Estanislao Goya	T77	Round 1	5	4	3	3	4	5	4	3	5	5	4	6	3	4	4	3	5	5	75
Argentina	**T132**	Round 2	4	5	5	3	5	5	3	6	5	4	4	4	4	4	5	6	5	4	81-**156**
Brendan Jones	T119	Round 1	4	4	5	3	4	4	4	4	5	4	3	5	4	4	5	4	7	5	78
Australia	**T132**	Round 2	4	4	5	4	5	4	3	4	6	4	4	4	3	5	5	4	6	4	78-**156**
Steven Fox*	T119	Round 1	4	4	4	4	5	4	4	4	7	4	4	5	4	5	4	3	5	4	78
USA	**T140**	Round 2	5	3	4	4	5	3	3	5	6	5	4	4	3	6	4	3	7	5	79-**157**
Matteo Manassero	T92	Round 1	5	4	4	4	3	4	3	6	6	4	4	4	5	4	3	5	4	76	
Italy	**T140**	Round 2	5	5	4	4	4	4	4	5	4	4	4	4	5	5	5	5	5	5	81-**157**
Daisuke Maruyama	T119	Round 1	5	4	6	4	5	5	3	5	5	4	3	4	3	5	4	4	5	4	78
Japan	**T140**	Round 2	5	4	4	3	4	5	3	5	4	5	4	6	3	3	6	3	5	7	79-**157**
Kiradech Aphibarnrat	T27	Round 1	4	5	4	2	4	4	3	4	5	3	5	4	3	4	5	4	5	4	72
Thailand	**T140**	Round 2	7	4	4	5	6	5	4	5	5	4	4	5	3	5	6	3	6	4	85-**157**
Brian Davis	T143	Round 1	5	4	4	3	5	5	4	4	7	4	4	6	4	4	4	3	5	5	80
England	**T140**	Round 2	4	4	4	4	5	4	3	4	6	5	4	3	4	5	5	3	5	5	77-**157**

HOLE			1	2	3	4	5	6	7	8	9	10	11	12	13	14	15	16	17	18	
PAR	POSITION		4	4	4	3	5	4	3	4	5	4	4	4	3	4	4	3	5	4	TOTAL
Sir Nick Faldo	T134	Round 1	5	5	3	3	5	4	4	3	6	4	4	4	4	6	4	4	7	4	79
England	**T140**	Round 2	4	4	5	3	6	4	3	4	5	3	6	4	4	5	4	3	5	6	78 -157
Luke Guthrie	T119	Round 1	7	5	4	3	6	4	3	4	5	3	3	4	3	5	5	4	6	4	78
USA	**146**	Round 2	5	4	6	3	6	4	3	6	4	4	5	4	2	4	5	5	6	4	80 -158
Grant Forrest*	T47	Round 1	5	4	4	2	5	6	3	4	4	5	4	4	4	5	3	2	5	4	73
Scotland	**T147**	Round 2	6	5	4	5	6	5	4	4	6	6	3	3	4	5	5	4	6	5	86 -159
Makoto Inoue	152	Round 1	4	4	5	6	5	5	4	6	5	5	4	4	3	5	4	3	6	5	83
Japan	**T147**	Round 2	4	4	4	3	7	4	2	4	4	4	5	4	5	5	4	4	5	4	76 -159
Scott Brown	T134	Round 1	5	5	4	4	4	5	3	4	7	5	5	4	4	4	3	4	5	4	79
USA	**149**	Round 2	6	4	4	3	5	5	3	6	5	5	4	3	5	5	5	4	5	4	81 -160
Rhys Pugh*	153	Round 1	5	4	4	3	5	4	3	4	6	4	4	5	4	5	5	7	7	5	84
Wales	**T150**	Round 2	5	4	4	2	5	4	3	4	5	5	5	4	4	4	7	4	5	3	77 -161
Satoshi Kodaira	T143	Round 1	4	3	4	4	4	6	3	5	9	4	4	4	5	5	4	3	5	4	80
Japan	**T150**	Round 2	5	4	4	3	5	5	3	5	6	5	4	6	3	5	4	4	5	5	81 -161
Tyrrell Hatton	T150	Round 1	6	3	5	3	6	4	4	4	7	6	3	4	3	4	6	3	5	6	82
England	**T150**	Round 2	5	5	5	4	6	5	2	4	5	4	4	4	3	4	4	3	6	6	79 -161
Scott Piercy	T59	Round 1	5	3	4	2	4	5	3	4	6	5	6	4	4	4	4	3	4	4	74
USA	**153**	Round 2	5	5	6	4	6	5	3	7	5	4	5	4	3	5	5	4	5	7	88 -162
Alexander Noren	T154	Round 1	6	5	4	3	5	4	3	4	6	6	4	5	4	5	5	4	4	6	83 WD
Sweden																					
Peter Hanson	T154	Round 1	6	5	4	3	4														WD
Sweden																					
Louis Oosthuizen	T154	Round 1	5	3	4	4	5	4	5	5											WD
South Africa																					

THE TOP TENS

Driving Distance

1. Gareth Wright 305.1
2. Stephen Gallacher 301.3
3. Mark Brown 297.9
4. Boo Weekley 296.9
5. Paul Lawrie 296.6
6. Bo Van Pelt 294.1
7. Keegan Bradley 293.9
8. Fredrik Jacobson 293.5
9. Rafael Cabrera-Bello 293.4
10. Jason Dufner 292.6
63. Phil Mickelson 275.0

Fairways Hit

Maximum of 56

1. Henrik Stenson 45
2. Adam Scott 44
2. Francesco Molinari 44
4. Chris Wood 43
5. Tiger Woods 42
6. Ryan Moore 40
6. Gregory Bourdy 40
6. Ken Duke 40
9. Shane Lowry 39
9. Matthew Fitzpatrick* 39
37. Phil Mickelson 34

Greens in Regulation

Maximum of 72

1. Henrik Stenson 57
2. Hideki Matsuyama 55
3. Chris Wood 51
3. Josh Teater 51
5. Tiger Woods 50
5. Ryan Moore 50
5. Jordan Spieth 50
5. Boo Weekley 50
9. Angel Cabrera 49
9. Bo Van Pelt 49
9. Tim Clark 49
9. Branden Grace 49
27. Phil Mickelson 46

Putts

1. Lee Westwood 110
2. Martin Laird 113
3. Harris English 115
4. Brandt Snedeker 116
4. Charl Schwartzel 116
4. YE Yang 116
7. Phil Mickelson 117
7. Fred Couples 117
9. Rafael Cabrera-Bello 118
9. Jason Day 118

Statistical Rankings

Name	Driving Distance	Rank	Fairways Hit	Rank	Greens In Regulation	Rank	Putts	Rank
Thomas Bjorn	275.0	63	23	82	39	79	123	29
Jonas Blixt	284.9	21	28	75	45	35	122	23
Gregory Bourdy	266.0	80	40	6	42	58	124	39
Keegan Bradley	293.9	7	31	57	43	51	120	16
Mark Brown	297.9	3	36	20	48	13	126	56
Angel Cabrera	278.3	39	37	16	49	9	125	46
Rafael Cabrera-Bello	293.4	9	22	83	39	79	118	9
Bud Cauley	284.5	24	33	45	42	58	120	16
KJ Choi	275.3	59	36	20	42	58	121	21
Stewart Cink	271.1	75	35	28	45	35	127	62
Tim Clark	275.1	62	38	11	49	9	133	81
Darren Clarke	275.3	59	34	37	48	13	121	21
George Coetzee	286.1	18	26	80	40	75	125	46
Fred Couples	283.8	26	24	81	37	84	117	7
Ben Curtis	278.1	42	32	52	48	13	128	68
Jason Day	277.8	48	35	28	40	75	118	9
Eduardo De La Riva	265.1	81	36	20	47	22	122	23
Graham DeLaet	275.6	58	34	37	42	58	127	62
Jamie Donaldson	263.0	83	35	28	48	13	126	56
Jason Dufner	292.6	10	35	28	46	27	125	46
Ken Duke	273.1	71	40	6	42	58	126	56
Ernie Els	274.4	67	29	73	42	58	122	23
Harris English	291.9	11	31	57	42	58	115	3
Gonzalo Fdez-Castano	286.1	18	31	57	44	42	125	46
Oliver Fisher	275.3	59	27	76	45	35	123	29
Matthew Fitzpatrick*	277.4	50	39	9	45	35	125	46
Marcus Fraser	272.9	73	30	67	41	69	123	29
Stephen Gallacher	301.3	2	36	20	44	42	122	23
Sergio Garcia	278.8	38	36	20	46	27	125	46
Branden Grace	279.3	36	31	57	49	9	126	56
Todd Hamilton	278.0	43	32	52	44	42	130	77
Padraig Harrington	284.5	24	38	11	46	27	129	73
Russell Henley	280.4	32	34	37	43	51	124	39
Mikko Ilonen	280.0	33	33	45	48	13	132	80
Fredrik Jacobson	293.5	8	33	45	42	58	125	46
Thongchai Jaidee	289.8	13	37	16	44	42	123	29
Miguel Angel Jimenez	263.1	82	33	45	41	69	119	11
Zach Johnson	278.3	39	37	16	47	22	120	16
Dustin Johnson	290.0	12	38	11	46	27	127	62
Shiv Kapur	274.3	68	33	45	43	51	124	39
Shingo Katayama	276.0	55	31	57	44	42	123	29
Martin Kaymer	261.6	84	34	37	45	35	127	62
KT Kim	277.9	45	37	16	44	42	126	56
Matt Kuchar	287.1	17	35	28	45	35	124	39
Martin Laird	288.0	14	32	52	38	81	113	2
Paul Lawrie	296.6	5	31	57	43	51	119	11
Tom Lehman	273.0	72	31	57	42	58	124	39
Justin Leonard	276.1	54	34	37	46	27	123	29
Shane Lowry	287.6	15	39	9	46	27	124	39
Sandy Lyle	278.3	39	27	76	38	81	125	46
Hunter Mahan	283.4	29	35	28	43	51	119	11
Hideki Matsuyama	274.3	68	35	28	55	2	129	73
Graeme McDowell	268.1	78	38	11	41	69	123	29
Phil Mickelson	275.0	63	34	37	46	27	117	7
Francesco Molinari	273.5	70	44	2	48	13	123	29
Ryan Moore	274.5	65	40	6	50	5	128	68
Jimmy Mullen*	268.4	77	32	52	38	81	120	16
Geoff Ogilvy	284.8	23	32	52	44	42	123	29
Mark O'Meara	279.3	36	29	73	47	22	127	62
Carl Pettersson	280.0	33	27	76	43	51	122	23
Ian Poulter	276.0	55	35	28	46	27	120	16
Richie Ramsay	277.6	49	36	20	42	58	125	46
Charl Schwartzel	285.4	20	36	20	40	75	116	4
Adam Scott	276.6	53	44	2	47	22	122	23
Peter Senior	280.0	33	38	11	42	58	129	73
Webb Simpson	271.5	74	31	57	48	13	130	77
Brandt Snedeker	276.9	51	30	67	41	69	116	4
Jordan Spieth	276.0	55	33	45	50	5	128	68
Henrik Stenson	277.9	45	45	1	57	1	127	62
Richard Sterne	283.6	28	34	37	48	13	125	46
Kevin Streelman	280.5	31	30	67	40	75	124	39
Josh Teater	282.1	30	21	84	51	3	137	84
Steven Tiley	267.4	79	36	20	41	69	119	11
Bo Van Pelt	294.1	6	34	37	49	9	129	73
Johnson Wagner	274.5	65	33	45	48	13	128	68
Bubba Watson	283.8	26	31	57	45	35	128	68
Boo Weekley	296.9	4	30	67	50	5	134	82
Lee Westwood	278.0	43	30	67	41	69	110	1
Bernd Wiesberger	284.9	21	31	57	43	51	126	56
Daniel Willett	287.5	16	27	76	47	22	119	11
Chris Wood	276.8	52	43	4	51	3	135	83
Tiger Woods	270.1	76	42	5	50	5	123	29
Gareth Wright	305.1	1	30	67	44	42	131	79
YE Yang	277.9	45	35	28	44	42	116	4

	Driving Distance	Rank	Fairways Hit	Rank	Greens In Regulation	Rank	Putts	Rank
Thomas Aiken	279.5	113	19	21	24	28	67	117
Kiradech Aphibarnrat	290.0	57	14	110	21	83	68	130
Scott Brown	279.5	113	18	33	19	118	67	117
Mark Calcavecchia	276.3	122	17	45	19	118	62	36
Nicolas Colsaerts	282.3	99	18	33	25	17	70	145
Stephen Dartnall	290.0	57	17	45	23	46	67	117
Brian Davis	274.5	128	15	97	17	142	64	69
Luke Donald	263.8	147	16	71	19	118	63	51
David Duval	257.5	152	7	152	15	151	62	36
Sir Nick Faldo	287.8	71	16	71	16	148	66	101
Niclas Fasth	297.8	24	14	110	18	130	60	16
Oscar Floren	277.3	118	16	71	26	10	68	130
Grant Forrest*	286.5	79	14	110	18	130	66	101
Rickie Fowler	294.0	44	14	110	21	83	69	139
Steven Fox*	273.8	130	15	97	18	130	64	69
Hiroyuki Fujita	267.0	143	15	97	23	46	65	80
Jim Furyk	286.3	81	17	45	23	46	68	130
Robert Garrigus	289.3	64	16	71	19	118	63	51
Lucas Glover	296.3	31	12	138	21	83	72	150
Estanislao Goya	301.8	17	14	110	20	105	66	101
Luke Guthrie	275.8	124	12	138	22	68	74	153
Bill Haas	295.8	34	16	71	21	83	65	80
Justin Harding	296.3	31	16	71	20	105	66	101
Tyrrell Hatton	281.5	103	10	149	17	142	62	36
Billy Horschel	297.3	26	16	71	19	118	65	80
John Huh	292.0	50	17	45	19	118	65	80
Makoto Inoue	267.8	141	16	71	19	118	69	139
Scott Jamieson	266.8	145	12	138	20	105	65	80
Steven Jeffress	287.3	74	22	4	20	105	66	101
Brendan Jones	304.3	11	9	150	13	153	62	36
Robert Karlsson	281.3	105	16	71	24	28	71	148
Hyung-Sung Kim	291.0	54	16	71	25	17	68	130
Satoshi Kodaira	285.3	86	13	125	16	148	65	80
Brooks Koepka	297.3	26	16	71	21	83	67	117
Kenichi Kuboya	289.8	62	16	71	17	142	65	80
Marc Leishman	282.0	100	17	45	24	28	66	101
Darryn Lloyd	300.8	18	13	125	23	46	68	130
David Lynn	285.5	85	13	125	18	130	67	117
Matteo Manassero	284.5	88	15	97	16	148	67	117
Daisuke Maruyama	280.3	109	20	16	22	68	68	130
Gareth Maybin	261.5	149	20	16	18	130	64	69
Richard McEvoy	280.3	109	18	33	23	46	70	145
Rory McIlroy	307.0	5	8	151	23	46	66	101
George Murray	259.5	151	17	45	21	83	63	51
Thorbjorn Olesen	289.3	64	17	45	22	68	67	117
Scott Piercy	305.8	8	5	153	14	152	63	51
DA Points	308.8	4	17	45	22	68	67	117
Garrick Porteous*	297.3	26	18	33	18	130	63	51
Rhys Pugh*	282.8	98	12	138	19	118	68	130
Alvaro Quiros	327.0	1	16	71	23	46	69	139
Justin Rose	298.3	21	15	97	25	17	70	145
Brett Rumford	286.0	84	15	97	17	142	63	51
Lloyd Saltman	284.0	92	12	138	18	130	62	36
John Senden	294.5	41	15	97	21	83	68	130
Marcel Siem	298.0	23	13	125	24	28	66	101
Vijay Singh	287.8	71	19	21	24	28	72	150
Scott Stallings	293.3	46	14	110	20	105	66	101
Kyle Stanley	304.5	9	14	110	25	17	65	80
Ben Stow*	267.3	142	12	138	18	130	62	36
Toru Taniguchi	277.8	116	17	45	19	118	64	69
Michael Thompson	276.5	121	18	33	18	130	61	25
Camilo Villegas	294.3	43	17	45	20	105	64	69
John Wade	288.5	68	18	33	22	68	65	80
Jimmy Walker	299.0	20	17	45	21	83	66	101
Marc Warren	295.8	34	13	125	17	142	60	16
Nick Watney	281.0	107	17	45	24	28	69	139
Tom Watson	255.3	153	16	71	19	118	64	69
Thaworn Wiratchant	290.8	55	14	110	17	142	66	101
Ashun Wu	276.0	123	19	21	26	10	72	150

Roll of Honour

Year	Champion	Score	Margin	Runners-up	Venue
1860	Willie Park Sr	174	2	Tom Morris Sr	Prestwick
1861	Tom Morris Sr	163	4	Willie Park Sr	Prestwick
1862	Tom Morris Sr	163	13	Willie Park Sr	Prestwick
1863	Willie Park Sr	168	2	Tom Morris Sr	Prestwick
1864	Tom Morris Sr	167	2	Andrew Strath	Prestwick
1865	Andrew Strath	162	2	Willie Park Sr	Prestwick
1866	Willie Park Sr	169	2	David Park	Prestwick
1867	Tom Morris Sr	170	2	Willie Park Sr	Prestwick
1868	Tommy Morris Jr	154	3	Tom Morris Sr	Prestwick
1869	Tommy Morris Jr	157	11	Bob Kirk	Prestwick
1870	Tommy Morris Jr	149	12	Bob Kirk, Davie Strath	Prestwick
1871	*No Competition*				
1872	Tommy Morris Jr	166	3	Davie Strath	Prestwick
1873	Tom Kidd	179	1	Jamie Anderson	St Andrews
1874	Mungo Park	159	2	Tommy Morris Jr	Musselburgh
1875	Willie Park Sr	166	2	Bob Martin	Prestwick
1876	Bob Martin	176	—	Davie Strath	St Andrews
	(Martin was awarded the title when Strath refused to play-off)				
1877	Jamie Anderson	160	2	Bob Pringle	Musselburgh
1878	Jamie Anderson	157	2	Bob Kirk	Prestwick
1879	Jamie Anderson	169	3	Jamie Allan, Andrew Kirkaldy	St Andrews
1880	Bob Ferguson	162	5	Peter Paxton	Musselburgh
1881	Bob Ferguson	170	3	Jamie Anderson	Prestwick
1882	Bob Ferguson	171	3	Willie Fernie	St Andrews
1883	Willie Fernie	158	Playoff	Bob Ferguson	Musselburgh
1884	Jack Simpson	160	4	Douglas Rolland, Willie Fernie	Prestwick
1885	Bob Martin	171	1	Archie Simpson	St Andrews
1886	David Brown	157	2	Willie Campbell	Musselburgh
1887	Willie Park Jr	161	1	Bob Martin	Prestwick
1888	Jack Burns	171	1	David Anderson Jr, Ben Sayers	St Andrews
1889	Willie Park Jr	155	Playoff	Andrew Kirkaldy	Musselburgh
1890	John Ball Jr*	164	3	Willie Fernie, Archie Simpson	Prestwick
1891	Hugh Kirkaldy	166	2	Willie Fernie, Andrew Kirkaldy	St Andrews
	(From 1892 the competition was extended to 72 holes)				
1892	Harold Hilton*	305	3	John Ball Jr*, Hugh Kirkaldy, Sandy Herd	Muirfield
1893	Willie Auchterlonie	322	2	John Laidlay*	Prestwick
1894	JH Taylor	326	5	Douglas Rolland	St George's
1895	JH Taylor	322	4	Sandy Herd	St Andrews
1896	Harry Vardon	316	Playoff	JH Taylor	Muirfield

James Braid, Muirfield Champion 1901, 1906

Gary Player, Muirfield Champion 1959

Jack Nicklaus, Muirfield Champion 1966

Year	Champion	Score	Margin	Runners-up	Venue
1897	Harold Hilton*	314	1	James Braid	Royal Liverpool
1898	Harry Vardon	307	1	Willie Park Jr	Prestwick
1899	Harry Vardon	310	5	Jack White	St George's
1900	JH Taylor	309	8	Harry Vardon	St Andrews
1901	James Braid	309	3	Harry Vardon	Muirfield
1902	Sandy Herd	307	1	Harry Vardon, James Braid	Royal Liverpool
1903	Harry Vardon	300	6	Tom Vardon	Prestwick
1904	Jack White	296	1	James Braid, JH Taylor	Royal St George's
1905	James Braid	318	5	JH Taylor, Rowland Jones	St Andrews
1906	James Braid	300	4	JH Taylor	Muirfield
1907	Arnaud Massy	312	2	JH Taylor	Royal Liverpool
1908	James Braid	291	8	Tom Ball	Prestwick
1909	JH Taylor	295	6	James Braid, Tom Ball	Cinque Ports
1910	James Braid	299	4	Sandy Herd	St Andrews
1911	Harry Vardon	303	Playoff	Arnaud Massy	Royal St George's
1912	Ted Ray	295	4	Harry Vardon	Muirfield
1913	JH Taylor	304	8	Ted Ray	Royal Liverpool
1914	Harry Vardon	306	3	JH Taylor	Prestwick
1915-1919 *No Championship*					
1920	George Duncan	303	2	Sandy Herd	Cinque Ports
1921	Jock Hutchison	296	Playoff	Roger Wethered*	St Andrews
1922	Walter Hagen	300	1	George Duncan, Jim Barnes	Royal St George's
1923	Arthur Havers	295	1	Walter Hagen	Troon
1924	Walter Hagen	301	1	Ernest Whitcombe	Royal Liverpool
1925	Jim Barnes	300	1	Archie Compston, Ted Ray	Prestwick
1926	Bobby Jones*	291	2	Al Watrous	Royal Lytham
1927	Bobby Jones*	285	6	Aubrey Boomer, Fred Robson	St Andrews
1928	Walter Hagen	292	2	Gene Sarazen	Royal St George's
1929	Walter Hagen	292	6	Johnny Farrell	Muirfield
1930	Bobby Jones*	291	2	Leo Diegel, Macdonald Smith	Royal Liverpool
1931	Tommy Armour	296	1	Jose Jurado	Carnoustie
1932	Gene Sarazen	283	5	Macdonald Smith	Prince's
1933	Denny Shute	292	Playoff	Craig Wood	St Andrews
1934	Henry Cotton	283	5	Sid Brews	Royal St George's

Year	Champion	Score	Margin	Runners-up	Venue
1935	Alf Perry	283	4	Alf Padgham	Muirfield
1936	Alf Padgham	287	1	Jimmy Adams	Royal Liverpool
1937	Henry Cotton	290	2	Reg Whitcombe	Carnoustie
1938	Reg Whitcombe	295	2	Jimmy Adams	Royal St George's
1939	Dick Burton	290	2	Johnny Bulla	St Andrews
1940-1945 No Championship					
1946	Sam Snead	290	4	Bobby Locke, Johnny Bulla	St Andrews
1947	Fred Daly	293	1	Reg Horne, Frank Stranahan*	Royal Liverpool
1948	Henry Cotton	284	5	Fred Daly	Muirfield
1949	Bobby Locke	283	Playoff	Harry Bradshaw	Royal St George's
1950	Bobby Locke	279	2	Roberto de Vicenzo	Troon
1951	Max Faulkner	285	2	Antonio Cerda	Royal Portrush
1952	Bobby Locke	287	1	Peter Thomson	Royal Lytham
1953	Ben Hogan	282	4	Frank Stranahan*, Dai Rees, Peter Thomson, Antonio Cerda	Carnoustie
1954	Peter Thomson	283	1	Syd Scott, Dai Rees, Bobby Locke	Royal Birkdale
1955	Peter Thomson	281	2	John Fallon	St Andrews
1956	Peter Thomson	286	3	Flory Van Donck	Royal Liverpool
1957	Bobby Locke	279	3	Peter Thomson	St Andrews
1958	Peter Thomson	278	Playoff	Dave Thomas	Royal Lytham
1959	Gary Player	284	2	Flory van Donck, Fred Bullock	Muirfield
1960	Kel Nagle	278	1	Arnold Palmer	St Andrews
1961	Arnold Palmer	284	1	Dai Rees	Royal Birkdale
1962	Arnold Palmer	276	6	Kel Nagle	Troon
1963	Bob Charles	277	Playoff	Phil Rodgers	Royal Lytham
1964	Tony Lema	279	5	Jack Nicklaus	St Andrews
1965	Peter Thomson	285	2	Christy O'Connor Sr, Brian Huggett	Royal Birkdale
1966	Jack Nicklaus	282	1	Dave Thomas, Doug Sanders	Muirfield
1967	Roberto de Vicenzo	278	2	Jack Nicklaus	Royal Liverpool
1968	Gary Player	289	2	Jack Nicklaus, Bob Charles	Carnoustie
1969	Tony Jacklin	280	2	Bob Charles	Royal Lytham
1970	Jack Nicklaus	283	Playoff	Doug Sanders	St Andrews
1971	Lee Trevino	278	1	Liang Huan Lu	Royal Birkdale
1972	Lee Trevino	278	1	Jack Nicklaus	Muirfield
1973	Tom Weiskopf	276	3	Neil Coles, Johnny Miller	Troon
1974	Gary Player	282	4	Peter Oosterhuis	Royal Lytham
1975	Tom Watson	279	Playoff	Jack Newton	Carnoustie
1976	Johnny Miller	279	6	Jack Nicklaus, Seve Ballesteros	Royal Birkdale
1977	Tom Watson	268	1	Jack Nicklaus	Turnberry
1978	Jack Nicklaus	281	2	Simon Owen, Ben Crenshaw, Ray Floyd, Tom Kite	St Andrews
1979	Seve Ballesteros	283	3	Jack Nicklaus, Ben Crenshaw	Royal Lytham
1980	Tom Watson	271	4	Lee Trevino	Muirfield
1981	Bill Rogers	276	4	Bernhard Langer	Royal St George's
1982	Tom Watson	284	1	Peter Oosterhuis, Nick Price	Royal Troon
1983	Tom Watson	275	1	Hale Irwin, Andy Bean	Royal Birkdale
1984	Seve Ballesteros	276	2	Bernhard Langer, Tom Watson	St Andrews
1985	Sandy Lyle	282	1	Payne Stewart	Royal St George's
1986	Greg Norman	280	5	Gordon J Brand	Turnberry
1987	Nick Faldo	279	1	Rodger Davis, Paul Azinger	Muirfield
1988	Seve Ballesteros	273	2	Nick Price	Royal Lytham
1989	Mark Calcavecchia	275	Playoff	Greg Norman, Wayne Grady	Royal Troon

Walter Hagen, Muirfield Champion 1929

Lee Trevino, Muirfield Champion 1972

Year	Champion	Score	Margin	Runners-up	Venue
1990	Nick Faldo	270	5	Mark McNulty, Payne Stewart	St Andrews
1991	Ian Baker-Finch	272	2	Mike Harwood	Royal Birkdale
1992	Nick Faldo	272	1	John Cook	Muirfield
1993	Greg Norman	267	2	Nick Faldo	Royal St George's
1994	Nick Price	268	1	Jesper Parnevik	Turnberry
1995	John Daly	282	Playoff	Costantino Rocca	St Andrews
1996	Tom Lehman	271	2	Mark McCumber, Ernie Els	Royal Lytham
1997	Justin Leonard	272	3	Jesper Parnevik, Darren Clarke	Royal Troon
1998	Mark O'Meara	280	Playoff	Brian Watts	Royal Birkdale
1999	Paul Lawrie	290	Playoff	Justin Leonard, Jean Van de Velde	Carnoustie
2000	Tiger Woods	269	8	Ernie Els, Thomas Bjorn	St Andrews
2001	David Duval	274	3	Niclas Fasth	Royal Lytham
2002	Ernie Els	278	Playoff	Thomas Levet, Stuart Appleby, Steve Elkington	Muirfield
2003	Ben Curtis	283	1	Thomas Bjorn, Vijay Singh	Royal St George's
2004	Todd Hamilton	274	Playoff	Ernie Els	Royal Troon
2005	Tiger Woods	274	5	Colin Montgomerie	St Andrews
2006	Tiger Woods	270	2	Chris DiMarco	Royal Liverpool
2007	Padraig Harrington	277	Playoff	Sergio Garcia	Carnoustie
2008	Padraig Harrington	283	4	Ian Poulter	Royal Birkdale
2009	Stewart Cink	278	Playoff	Tom Watson	Turnberry
2010	Louis Oosthuizen	272	7	Lee Westwood	St Andrews
2011	Darren Clarke	275	3	Phil Mickelson, Dustin Johnson	Royal St George's
2012	Ernie Els	273	1	Adam Scott	Royal Lytham
2013	Phil Mickelson	281	3	Henrik Stenson	Muirfield

*Denotes amateurs

Records

Most Victories

6: Harry Vardon, 1896, 1898, 1899, 1903, 1911, 1914
5: James Braid, 1901, 1905, 1906, 1908, 1910; JH Taylor, 1894, 1895, 1900, 1909, 1913; Peter Thomson, 1954, 1955, 1956, 1958, 1965; Tom Watson, 1975, 1977, 1980, 1982, 1983

Most Runner-Up or Joint Runner-Up Finishes

7: Jack Nicklaus, 1964, 1967, 1968, 1972, 1976, 1977, 1979
6: JH Taylor, 1896, 1904, 1905, 1906, 1907, 1914

Oldest Winners

Tom Morris Sr, 1867, 46 years 102 days
Roberto de Vicenzo, 1967, 44 years 92 days
Harry Vardon, 1914, 44 years 41 days
Tom Morris Sr, 1864, 43 years 92 days
Phil Mickelson, 2013, 43 years 35 days
Darren Clarke, 2011, 42 years 337 days
Ernie Els, 2012, 42 years 279 days

Youngest Winners

Tommy Morris Jr, 1868, 17 years 156 days
Tommy Morris Jr, 1869, 18 years 149 days
Tommy Morris Jr, 1870, 19 years 148 days
Willie Auchterlonie, 1893, 21 years 22 days
Tommy Morris Jr, 1872, 21 years 146 days
Seve Ballesteros, 1979, 22 years 103 days

Known Oldest and Youngest Competitors

74 years, 11 months, 24 days: Tom Morris Sr, 1896
74 years, 4 months, 9 days: Gene Sarazen, 1976
14 years, 4 months, 25 days: Tommy Morris Jr, 1865

Largest Margin of Victory

13 strokes, Tom Morris Sr, 1862
12 strokes, Tommy Morris Jr, 1870
11 strokes, Tommy Morris Jr, 1869
8 strokes, JH Taylor, 1900 and 1913; James Braid, 1908; Tiger Woods, 2000

Lowest Winning Total by a Champion

267, Greg Norman, Royal St George's 1993 – 66, 68, 69, 64

268, Tom Watson, Turnberry, 1977 – 68, 70, 65, 65; Nick Price, Turnberry, 1994 – 69, 66, 67, 66
269, Tiger Woods, St Andrews, 2000 – 67, 66, 67, 69

Lowest Total in Relation to Par Since 1963

19 under par: Tiger Woods, St Andrews, 2000 (269)
18 under par: Nick Faldo, St Andrews, 1990 (270); Tiger Woods, Royal Liverpool, 2006 (270)

Lowest Total by a Runner-Up

269: Jack Nicklaus, Turnberry, 1977 – 68, 70, 65, 66; Nick Faldo, Royal St George's, 1993 – 69, 63, 70, 67; Jesper Parnevik, Turnberry, 1994 – 68, 66, 68, 67

Lowest Total by an Amateur

281: Iain Pyman, Royal St George's, 1993 – 68, 72, 70, 71; Tiger Woods, Royal Lytham & St Annes, 1996 – 75, 66, 70, 70

Lowest Individual Round

63: Mark Hayes, second round, Turnberry, 1977; Isao Aoki, third round, Muirfield, 1980; Greg Norman, second round, Turnberry, 1986; Paul Broadhurst, third round, St Andrews, 1990; Jodie Mudd, fourth round, Royal Birkdale, 1991; Nick Faldo, second round, Royal St George's, 1993; Payne Stewart, fourth round, Royal St George's, 1993; Rory McIlroy, first round, St Andrews, 2010

Lowest Individual Round by an Amateur

65: Tom Lewis, first round, Royal St George's, 2011

Lowest First Round

63: Rory McIlroy, St Andrews, 2010

Lowest Second Round

63: Mark Hayes, Turnberry, 1977; Greg Norman, Turnberry, 1986; Nick Faldo, Royal St George's, 1993

Lowest Third Round

63: Isao Aoki, Muirfield, 1980; Paul Broadhurst, St Andrews, 1990

Lowest Fourth Round

63: Jodie Mudd, Royal Birkdale, 1991; Payne Stewart, Royal St George's, 1993

Lowest Score over the First 36 Holes

130: Nick Faldo, Muirfield, 1992 – 66, 64; Brandt Snedeker, Royal Lytham & St Annes, 2012 – 66, 64

Lowest Score over the Middle 36 Holes

130: Fuzzy Zoeller, Turnberry, 1994 – 66, 64

Lowest Score over the Final 36 Holes

130: Tom Watson, Turnberry, 1977 – 65, 65; Ian Baker-Finch, Royal Birkdale, 1991 – 64, 66; Anders Forsbrand, Turnberry, 1994 – 66, 64

Lowest Score over the First 54 Holes

198: Tom Lehman, Royal Lytham & St Annes, 1996 – 67, 67, 64
199: Nick Faldo, St Andrews, 1990 – 67, 65, 67; Nick Faldo, Muirfield, 1992 – 66, 64, 69; Adam Scott, Royal Lytham, 2012 – 64, 67, 68

Lowest Score over the Final 54 Holes

199: Nick Price, Turnberry, 1994 – 66, 67, 66

Lowest Score for Nine Holes

28: Denis Durnian, first nine, Royal Birkdale, 1983
29: Tom Haliburton, first nine, Royal Lytham & St Annes, 1963; Peter Thomson, first nine, Royal Lytham & St Annes, 1963; Tony Jacklin, first nine, St Andrews, 1970; Bill Longmuir, first nine, Royal Lytham & St Annes, 1979; David J Russell first nine, Royal Lytham & St Annes, 1988; Ian Baker-Finch, first nine, St Andrews, 1990; Paul Broadhurst, first nine, St Andrews, 1990; Ian Baker-Finch, first nine, Royal Birkdale, 1991; Paul McGinley, first nine, Royal Lytham & St Annes, 1996; Ernie Els, first nine, Muirfield, 2002; Sergio Garcia, first nine, Royal Liverpool, 2006

Most Successive Victories

4: Tommy Morris Jr, 1868-72 *(No Championship in 1871)*
3: Jamie Anderson, 1877-79; Bob Ferguson, 1880-82; Peter Thomson, 1954-56
2: Tom Morris Sr, 1861-62; JH Taylor, 1894-95; Harry Vardon, 1898-99; James Braid, 1905-06; Bobby Jones, 1926-27; Walter Hagen, 1928-29; Bobby Locke, 1949-50; Arnold Palmer, 1961-62; Lee Trevino, 1971-72; Tom Watson, 1982-83; Tiger Woods, 2005-06; Padraig Harrington, 2007-08

Amateurs Who Have Won The Open

3: Bobby Jones, Royal Lytham & St Annes, 1926; St Andrews, 1927; Royal Liverpool, 1930
2: Harold Hilton, Muirfield, 1892; Royal Liverpool, 1897
1: John Ball Jr, Prestwick, 1890

Champions Who Won on Debut

Willie Park Sr, Prestwick, 1860; Tom Kidd, St Andrews, 1873; Mungo Park, Musselburgh, 1874; Jock Hutchison, St Andrews, 1921; Denny Shute, St Andrews, 1933; Ben Hogan, Carnoustie, 1953; Tony Lema, St Andrews, 1964; Tom Watson, Carnoustie, 1975; Ben Curtis, Royal St George's, 2003

Greatest Interval Between First and Last Victory

19 years: JH Taylor, 1894-1913
18 years: Harry Vardon, 1896-1914
15 years: Willie Park Sr, 1860-75; Gary Player, 1959-74
14 years: Henry Cotton, 1934-48

Greatest Interval Between Victories

11 years: Henry Cotton, 1937-48 *(No Championship 1940-45)*
10 years: Ernie Els, 2002-12
9 years: Willie Park Sr, 1866-75; Bob Martin, 1876-85; JH Taylor, 1900-09; Gary Player, 1959-68

Attendance

Year	Total
1960	39,563
1961	21,708
1962	37,098
1963	24,585
1964	35,954
1965	32,927
1966	40,182
1967	29,880
1968	51,819
1969	46,001
1970	81,593
1971	70,076
1972	84,746
1973	78,810
1974	92,796
1975	85,258
1976	92,021
1977	87,615
1978	125,271
1979	134,501
1980	131,610
1981	111,987
1982	133,299
1983	142,892
1984	193,126
1985	141,619
1986	134,261
1987	139,189
1988	191,334
1989	160,639
1990	208,680
1991	189,435
1992	146,427
1993	141,000
1994	128,000
1995	180,000
1996	170,000
1997	176,000
1998	195,100
1999	157,000
2000	230,000
2001	178,000
2002	161,500
2003	183,000
2004	176,000
2005	223,000
2006	230,000
2007	154,000
2008	201,500
2009	123,000
2010	201,000
2011	180,100
2012	181,300
2013	142,036

Champions Who Have Won in Three Separate Decades

Harry Vardon, 1896, 1898 & 1899/1903/1911 & 1914
JH Taylor, 1894 & 1895/1900 & 1909/1913
Gary Player, 1959, 1968, 1974

Competitors with the Most Top Five Finishes

16: JH Taylor; Jack Nicklaus

Competitors Who Have Recorded the Most Rounds Under Par From 1963

59: Jack Nicklaus
53: Nick Faldo

Competitors with the Most Finishes Under Par From 1963

14: Jack Nicklaus; Nick Faldo; Ernie Els
13: Tom Watson

Champions Who Have Led Outright After Every Round

72 hole Championships
Ted Ray, 1912; Bobby Jones, 1927; Gene Sarazen, 1932; Henry Cotton, 1934; Tom Weiskopf, 1973; Tiger Woods, 2005
36 hole Championships
Willie Park Sr, 1860 and 1866; Tom Morris Sr, 1862 and 1864; Tommy Morris Jr, 1869 and 1870; Mungo Park, 1874; Jamie Anderson, 1879; Bob Ferguson, 1880, 1881, 1882; Willie Fernie, 1883; Jack Simpson, 1884; Hugh Kirkaldy, 1891

Largest Leads Since 1892

After 18 holes:
5 strokes: Sandy Herd, 1896
4 strokes: Harry Vardon, 1902; Jim Barnes, 1925; Christy O'Connor Jr, 1985
After 36 holes:
9 strokes: Henry Cotton, 1934
6 strokes: Abe Mitchell, 1920
After 54 holes:
10 strokes: Henry Cotton, 1934
7 strokes: Harry Vardon, 1903; Tony Lema, 1964
6 strokes: JH Taylor, 1900; James Braid, 1905; James Braid, 1908; Max Faulkner, 1951; Tom Lehman, 1996; Tiger Woods, 2000

Champions Who Had Four Rounds, Each Better than the One Before

Jack White, Royal St George's, 1904 – 80, 75, 72, 69
James Braid, Muirfield, 1906 – 77, 76, 74, 73
Ben Hogan, Carnoustie, 1953 – 73, 71, 70, 68
Gary Player, Muirfield, 1959 – 75, 71, 70, 68

Same Number of Strokes in Each of the Four Rounds by a Champion

Denny Shute, St Andrews, 1933 – 73, 73, 73, 73 (excluding the playoff)

Best 18-Hole Recovery by a Champion

George Duncan, Deal, 1920. Duncan was 13 strokes behind the leader, Abe Mitchell, after 36 holes and level with him after 54.

Greatest Variation Between Rounds by a Champion

14 strokes: Henry Cotton, 1934, second round 65, fourth round 79
12 strokes: Henry Cotton, 1934, first round 67, fourth round 79
11 strokes: Jack White, 1904, first round 80, fourth round 69; Greg Norman, 1986, first round 74, second round 63; Greg Norman, 1986, second round 63, third round 74
10 strokes: Seve Ballesteros, 1979, second round 65, third round 75

Greatest Variation Between Two Successive Rounds by a Champion

11 strokes: Greg Norman, 1986, first round 74, second round 63; Greg Norman, 1986, second round 63, third round 74
10 strokes: Seve Ballesteros, 1979, second round 65, third round 75

Greatest Comeback by a Champion

After 18 holes
Harry Vardon, 1896, 11 strokes behind the leader
After 36 holes
George Duncan, 1920, 13 strokes behind the leader
After 54 holes
Paul Lawrie, 1999, 10 strokes behind the leader

Champions Who Had Four Rounds Under 70

Greg Norman, Royal St George's, 1993 – 66, 68, 69, 64; Nick Price, Turnberry, 1994 – 69, 66, 67, 66; Tiger Woods, St Andrews, 2000 – 67, 66, 67, 69

Competitors Who Failed to Win The Open Despite Having Four Rounds Under 70

Ernie Els, Royal St George's, 1993 – 68, 69, 69, 68; Jesper Parnevik, Turnberry, 1994 – 68, 66, 68, 67; Ernie Els, Royal Troon, 2004 – 69, 69, 68, 68

Lowest Final Round by a Champion

64: Greg Norman, Royal St George's, 1993
65: Tom Watson, Turnberry, 1977; Seve Ballesteros, Royal Lytham & St Annes, 1988; Justin Leonard, Royal Troon, 1997

Worst Round by a Champion Since 1939

78: Fred Daly, third round, Royal Liverpool, 1947
76: Bobby Locke, second round, Royal St George's, 1949; Paul Lawrie, third round, Carnoustie, 1999

Champion with the Worst Finishing Round Since 1939

75: Sam Snead, St Andrews, 1946

Lowest Opening Round by a Champion

65: Louis Oosthuizen, St Andrews, 2010

Most Open Championship Appearances

46: Gary Player
38: Jack Nicklaus, Sandy Lyle

Most Final Day Appearances Since 1892

32: Jack Nicklaus
31: Sandy Herd
30: JH Taylor
28: Ted Ray
27: Harry Vardon; James Braid; Nick Faldo
26: Peter Thomson; Gary Player

Most Appearances by a Champion Before His First Victory

19: Darren Clarke, 2011; Phil Mickelson, 2013
15: Nick Price, 1994
14: Sandy Herd, 1902

13: Ted Ray, 1912; Jack White, 1904; Reg Whitcombe, 1938; Mark O'Meara, 1998
11: George Duncan, 1920; Nick Faldo, 1987; Ernie Els, 2002; Stewart Cink, 2009
10: Roberto de Vicenzo, 1967; Padraig Harrington, 2007

The Open Which Provided the Greatest Number of Rounds Under 70 Since 1946

148 rounds, Turnberry, 1994

The Open with the Fewest Rounds Under 70 Since 1946

2 rounds, St Andrews, 1946; Royal Liverpool, 1947; Carnoustie, 1968

Statistically Most Difficult Hole Since 1982

St Andrews, 1984, Par-4 17th, 4.79

Longest Course in Open History

Carnoustie, 2007, 7,421 yards

Number of Times Each Course Has Hosted The Open Championship

St Andrews, 28; Prestwick, 24; Muirfield, 16; Royal St George's, 14; Royal Liverpool and Royal Lytham & St Annes, 11; Royal Birkdale, 9; Royal Troon, 8; Carnoustie, 7; Musselburgh, 6; Turnberry, 4; Royal Cinque Ports, 2; Royal Portrush and Prince's, 1

Prize Money (£)

Year	Total	First Prize	Year	Total	First Prize	Year	Total	First Prize	Year	Total	First Prize
1860	nil	nil	1889	22	8	1963	8,500	1,500	1990	825,000	85,000
1863	10	nil	1890	29.50	13	1965	10,000	1,750	1991	900,000	90,000
1864	15	6	1891	28.50	10	1966	15,000	2,100	1992	950,000	95,000
1865	20	8	1892	110	35	1968	20,000	3,000	1993	1,000,000	100,000
1866	11	6	1893	100	30	1969	30,000	4,250	1994	1,100,000	110,000
1867	16	7	1900	125	50	1970	40,000	5,250	1995	1,250,000	125,000
1868	12	6	1910	135	50	1971	45,000	5,500	1996	1,400,000	200,000
1872	unknown	8	1920	225	75	1972	50,000	5,500	1997	1,600,000	250,000
1873	unknown	11	1927	275	75	1975	75,000	7,500	1998	1,800,000	300,000
1874	20	8	1930	400	100	1977	100,000	10,000	1999	2,000,000	350,000
1876	27	10	1931	500	100	1978	125,000	12,500	2000	2,750,000	500,000
1877	20	8	1946	1,000	150	1979	155,000	15,000	2001	3,300,000	600,000
1878	unknown	8	1949	1,500	300	1980	200,000	25,000	2002	3,800,000	700,000
1879	47	10	1951	1,700	300	1982	250,000	32,000	2003	3,900,000	700,000
1880	unknown	8	1953	2,500	500	1983	310,000	40,000	2004	4,000,000	720,000
1881	21	8	1954	3,500	750	1984	451,000	55,000	2007	4,200,000	750,000
1882	47.25	12	1955	3,750	1,000	1985	530,000	65,000	2010	4,800,000	850,000
1883	20	8	1958	4,850	1,000	1986	600,000	70,000	2011	5,000,000	900,000
1884	23	8	1959	5,000	1,000	1987	650,000	75,000	2013	5,250,000	945,000
1885	35.50	10	1960	7,000	1,250	1988	700,000	80,000			
1886	20	8	1961	8,500	1,400	1989	750,000	80,000			

MUIRFIELD

142ND OPEN CHAMPIONSHIP
Card of the Championship Course

Hole	Par	Yards	Hole	Par	Yards
1	4	447	10	4	469
2	4	364	11	4	387
3	4	377	12	4	379
4	3	226	13	3	190
5	5	559	14	4	475
6	4	461	15	4	448
7	3	184	16	3	186
8	4	441	17	5	575
9	5	554	18	4	470
Out	36	3,613	In	35	3,579
			Total	71	7,192